CARRY
THE
FLAME

A BIBLE STUDY ON RENEWING YOUR HEART
AND REVIVING THE WORLD

STUDY GUIDE | FIVE SESSIONS

JIM CYMBALA

WITH REBECCA ENGLISH LAWSON

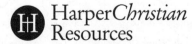
HarperChristian
Resources

Carry the Flame Study Guide
© 2023 Jim Cymbala

Requests for information should be addressed to:
HarperChristian Resources, 3900 Sparks Dr. SE, Grand Rapids, Michigan 49546

ISBN: 978-0-310-16075-5 (softcover)
ISBN: 978-0-310-16076-2 (e-book)

HarperChristian Resources titles may be purchased in bulk for church, business, fundraising, or ministry use. For information, please e-mail ResourceSpecialist@ChurchSource.com.

Published in association with the literary agency of Ann Spangler & Company 1415 Laurel Ave. SE, Grand Rapids, MI 49506.

First printing February 2023 / Printed in the United States of America

23 24 25 26 27 LBC 5 4 3 2 1

CONTENTS

SESSION 4: KEEP ON BEING FILLED

SESSION 5: THE HOLY SPIRIT STILL SPEAKS

A NOTE FROM JIM CYMBALA

It's a sad reality, but the church in America today is in a place not founded in the New Testament. The system in most churches seems to be, "You, the clergy, do all the work. We, the churchgoers, will sit in the pew, and if you're fortunate, we'll come to church a couple times a month." Sure, we love the Lord. We've put our faith in him. But many of us are content just to sit in church on Sunday and leave the work of ministry to the leaders.

Jesus did not suffer on a cross for six hours so we could go to church once a week! No, he died so we would be saved . . . and then he rose from the dead, ascended into heaven, and poured out the Holy Spirit on the early church. Why? So he could send people out to *carry the flame* of the gospel into a world that is in need of his light and love. He did not pour out his Spirit on just the twelve apostles. He used many others to do the work of ministry—men and women who never went to seminary, were not ordained ministers, were not famous personalities. He used everyday folks who had one thing in common: they were available.

I recently wrote a book called *Fan the Flame* to encourage pastors and leaders to persevere in their ministry of spreading the gospel. Now, in this Bible study, I want to inspire *you* to do the same. Often, we're tempted to sit back and say, "God can't use me. I'm too old. I'm too young. I'm not educated enough. I don't know enough Bible verses." God wants to dispel that kind of thinking. He can use little children. He can use the newest believer. He can use a person who dropped out of school in the third grade. We look at people and think, "Impossible!" But today, God is using ordinary, everyday people to build his kingdom.

So, you and I need to take a hard look—an honest look—inside ourselves and our churches. One day everything we own will be gone, and we will stand before the Lord of the harvest and have to give an account of what we did with the salvation he gave us. Did we share it? Did we serve him? Or did we just leave it all up to our leaders?

The people on the platform were never intended to do *all* the work of the Lord. There are too many people today who need to hear about Christ to leave it to the few who have seminary degrees and titles in the church. God has chosen each of us to play our part in his kingdom. So give yourself to the Lord Jesus. You have no idea what God can do through you if the flame of his Spirit touches your heart and you are yielded to his will.

— Jim Cymbala

HOW TO USE THIS GUIDE

If you think you're too inexperienced or not "qualified" enough to be used by God . . . think again. God has called *every* believer to serve him. He sent his Holy Spirit to empower *you* to do whatever assignment he has given you. With God, nothing is impossible.

In this study, you will look at the stories of ordinary people—most from the book of Acts—whom God used in extraordinary ways to carry the flame of the gospel. Each person was different. Each person was called to serve the Lord in unique ways. But every one of them was available to God. They simply wanted to be at his disposal. The same is true today. God is still looking for people who are open to hearing from him and willing to obey.

Before you begin this study, keep in mind there are few ways you can go through this material. You can experience the study with others in a small group (such as a Bible study, Sunday school class, or home group), or you may choose to go through the content on your own. Either way, the videos for each session are available for you to view at any time by following the instructions provided on the inside cover of this study guide.

Group Study

Each of the sessions in this study are divided into two parts: (1) a group study section, and (2) a personal study section. The group study section provides a basic framework on how to open your time together, get the most out of the video content, and discuss the key ideas together that were presented in the teaching. Each session includes the following:

- **Welcome:** A short note about the topic of the session for you to read on your own before you meet as a group.
- **Connect:** A few icebreaker questions to get you and your group members thinking about the topic and interacting with each other.
- **Watch:** An outline of the key points covered in each video teaching to help you follow along, stay engaged, and take notes.
- **Discuss:** Questions to help your group reflect on the teaching material presented and apply it to your lives. In each session, you will be given four suggested questions and four additional questions to use as time allows.

- **Respond:** A short personal exercise to help reinforce the key ideas.
- **Pray:** A place for you to record prayer requests and praises for the week.

If you are doing this study in a group, make sure you have your own copy of the study guide so you can write down your thoughts, responses, and reflections—and so you will have access to the videos via streaming. Finally, keep these points in mind:

- **Facilitation:** If you are doing this study in a group, you will want to appoint someone to serve as a facilitator. This person will be responsible for starting the video and keeping track of time during discussions and activities. If *you* have been chosen for this role, there are some resources in the back of this guide that can help you lead your group through the study.

- **Faithfulness:** Your group is a place where tremendous growth can happen as you reflect on the Bible, ask questions, learn what God is doing in other people's lives, and draw near to Jesus together. For this reason, be fully committed and attend each session so you can build trust and rapport with the other members.

- **Friendship:** The goal of any small group is to serve as a place where people can share, grow in the Lord together, and build friendships. So make your group a "safe place." Be honest about your thoughts and feelings, but also listen carefully to everyone else's thoughts, feelings, and opinions. Keep anything personal that your group members share in confidence so that you can create a community where people can heal, be challenged, and grow spiritually.

If you are going through this study on your own, read the opening Welcome section and reflect on the questions in the Connect section. Watch the video and use the prompts provided to take notes. Finally, personalize the questions and exercises in the Discuss and Respond sections. Close by recording any requests you want to pray about during the week.

Personal Study

The personal study is for you to work through on your own during the week. Each exercise is designed to help you explore the key ideas you uncovered during your group time and delve into passages of Scripture that will help you apply those principles to your life. Go at your own pace, doing a little each day—or tackle the material all at once. Remember to spend a few moments in silence to listen to what the Holy Spirit might be saying to you.

Each study session contains five days of exercises. On each of the five days, you will find a short devotional to read followed by a few verses of Scripture to help you dig into a key topic from that week's video. You will also engage in a few questions and exercises designed to help you apply the truths of the Scripture to your own life.

Note that if you are doing this study as part of a group and are unable to finish (or even start) these personal studies for the week, you should still attend the group time. Be assured that you are wanted and welcome even if you don't have your "homework" done. The group studies and personal studies are intended to help you hear what God wants to say to you and how to apply what he is saying to your life. So as you go through this study, be listening for him to speak to you as you learn what it means to carry the flame of God's love to the world.

SCHEDULE

WEEK 1

BEFORE GROUP MEETING	Read the Welcome section (page 3)
GROUP MEETING	Discuss the Connect questions Watch the video teaching for session 1 Discuss the questions that follow as a group Do the closing exercise and pray (pages 3–8)
PERSONAL STUDY – DAY 1	Complete the daily study (pages 10–11)
PERSONAL STUDY – DAY 2	Complete the daily study (pages 12–14)
PERSONAL STUDY – DAY 3	Complete the daily study (pages 15–16)
PERSONAL STUDY – DAY 4	Complete the daily study (pages 17–18)
PERSONAL STUDY – DAY 5 (before week 2 group meeting)	Complete the daily study (pages 19–21)

GOD USES ORDINARY PEOPLE

*After these things the Lord appointed seventy others also,
and sent them two by two before His face into every city and place
where He Himself was about to go. Then He said to them, "The harvest
truly is great, but the laborers are few; therefore pray the Lord of the
harvest to send out laborers into His harvest."*

LUKE 10:1–2 NKJV

Welcome | READ ON YOUR OWN

In this study, we will be looking primarily at stories of people in the book of Acts who made themselves available to the Holy Spirit. But in this first session, we are going to look at some people—seventy of them—whose story is found in the Gospels.[1]

One day, as Jesus went about ministering, he called seventy people to assist him. Their assignment was to go, in groups of two, to all the towns and places where he was about to go. They were to pave the way for Jesus—to tell people about him, love them, and help them.

God wants to use us in the same way. No matter where we live, there are people who are lonely, empty, and afraid. Jesus calls us to go before him into their lives, tell them about the salvation he offers, and manifest through our lives his love and compassion for them.

The seventy people whom Jesus sent out didn't represent the apostles or church leaders. They were just ordinary disciples who were born again through the Holy Spirit as they believed the message of the cross. It's unlikely they were scholars who could recite the Bible (which at this time was just the Old Testament) to support their points. They just knew Jesus had saved them.

When Jesus gave this assignment to these seventy people, they could have said, "I'm not ready," or, "I don't know enough Scripture," or, "I'm just a new Christian—send one of the disciples like Peter or John." But they understood that Jesus had called them to do a job, and they believed that he would equip them with the tools they needed to do it.

God isn't looking for *ability* among his people, he's looking for *availability*. He wants us to step out in faith and do what he's calling us to do. He wants us to carry the flame of his love into people's lives.

Connect | 15 MINUTES

If any of your group members don't know each other, take a few minutes to introduce yourselves. Then, to get things started, discuss one of the following questions:

- What is your primary goal or hope for participating in this study? (In other words, why are you here?)

— *or* —

- What is something you have done recently to bless someone else?

Watch | 20 MINUTES

Now watch the video for this session, which you can access by playing the DVD or through streaming (see the instructions provided on the inside front cover). As you watch, use the following outline to record any thoughts or concepts that stand out to you.

Outline

I. God calls ordinary people to carry the flame of his light and love to others.
   A. The seventy people Jesus sent out were not ordained, famous, or likely highly educated. They are never even named in the Bible.
   B. This shows us that God can use anonymous people, or people who don't know a lot of Scripture, to do his work. He simply wants people who are available to him.

II. We are called to pave the way for Jesus in people's lives.
   A. God wants us to do more than go to church once a week. He wants us to be available 24/7.
   B. Going before Jesus means paving the way for him to come into people's lives.

III. The fields are ripe unto harvest. In other words, people need Jesus.
   A. The harvest was an urgent matter to Jesus. He urged the seventy to tell people about him.
   B. The harvest field is made up of every race, background, age, economic status, and culture.

IV. The laborers are few. Too many Christians are letting the leaders do the work of ministry.
   A. Most of us settle for "I just go to church on Sundays." But Jesus is saying, "You've got to get out there and love people—because the laborers are few!"
   B. God is sovereign, yet he chooses to spread the gospel through ordinary people.
   C. People are lonely, empty, broken, and afraid to die. Jesus is sending us to them.

V. When we step out in faith to share Christ's love, God will equip us.
   A. The seventy didn't have the New Testament yet; they just had Jesus' verbal teaching. God can do the impossible through us when we are available to him.
   B. Jesus is the head of the church, and we are the body. A healthy body obeys the head.
   C. We don't have to worry about what to say. God will give us the words to minister to people.
   D. Jesus hung on a cross for us. So let's consecrate our lives to him! Let's be available to carry the flame of his love to the people around us.

Notes

Discuss | 35 MINUTES

Take some time to discuss what you just watched by answering the following questions. There are some suggested questions below that will help you begin your discussion, but feel free to pick any of the additional questions as well as time allows.

Suggested Questions

1. In Luke 10:1, we read, "The Lord appointed seventy others also, and sent them two by two before His face into every city and place where He Himself was about to go" (NKJV). Take a moment to read verses 3–12. What are some of the instructions that Jesus gave to these seventy individuals? What were some of their assignments?

2. When Jesus told these seventy that "the harvest is plentiful" (verse 2) he was saying that people were in need of his love. Who is someone you know who is hurting, empty, lonely, or fearful? How might God be calling you to minister to that person?

3. Consider this statement from the teaching: "We have to be available and have the simple faith to step out like the seventy disciples did. They just went and did what God told them. The miracle happens, the blessing comes, when you do what God tells you." What blessings have you received simply by making yourself available to God?

4. Often times, God does not reveal the entire plan to us when he calls us to take a step of faith. We have to take the first step of obedience, and then God shows us the next step. What step of faith do you sense that God is calling you to take today?

Additional Questions

5. Think about some of the people who have carried the flame of the gospel into your life. Who are some of these ordinary people who helped pave the way for *you* to know Jesus? What was it about them that drew you to the Lord? How can their lives inspire you to share Jesus with others the way they did with you?

6. What is your biggest obstacle to sharing the love of Christ with other people—fear, not feeling ready, not having the right training, being a new Christian, being too busy, simply not wanting to? How can God help you face this obstacle head on and overcome it?

7. God is sovereign and all-powerful. He doesn't need our resources or anything we can bring to accomplish his purposes in this world. Yet, he *chooses* to use us! Why do you think God desires to partner with us in his mission to bring lost people to himself?

8. Consider this statement from the teaching: "It's not ability that God is looking for . . . it's availability." What does it mean for you to be available to God?

Respond | 10 MINUTES

Take a few moments to reflect on this truth that God doesn't want your *ability*, he just wants our *availability*. Review the outline for the video teaching and any notes you took. Use the following questions to write down your most significant takeaways from this session.

What spoke most to your heart from the video teaching?

What do you sense God is stirring you to do as a result?

How will this impact your service to others this week?

Pray | 10 MINUTES

Praying for one another is one of the most important things you can do as a community. So use this time wisely and make it more than just a "closing prayer" to end your group. Be intentional about sharing prayer requests, reviewing how God is answering your prayers, and praying for each other as a group. Use the space below to write down any requests so that you and your group members can continue to pray about them in the week ahead.

Name	Request

PERSONAL STUDY

Every believer in Christ has a work assignment. Whether you recognize it or not, God has gifted you in unique ways to take the gospel to the people around you. This week, you will have the chance to explore a few passages of Scripture to see how God uses ordinary people to accomplish extraordinary things for him in this world. As you work through these exercises, be sure to write down your responses to the questions, as you will be given a few minutes to share your insights at the start of the next session if you are doing this study with others.

DAY 1

GOD IS CALLING YOU

When Jesus called seventy people to go ahead of him into all the places where he was about to go, he chose *ordinary* people. They were like us—not famous, not trained for ministry, not highly educated—yet still important to Jesus. He wanted them to pave the way for him.

God has a calling for every single follower of Christ. The problem is that we sometimes think the work of the gospel is only for pastors, leaders, or really "talented" people. We think we're not equipped to do anything great for God.

Think about this in your life. Maybe you're from a small town with little opportunities. Maybe you've never been to college. Maybe you've been beaten down by sorrow or hardship or failure and think that God couldn't possibly use you. Maybe you're young, or your family thinks your ideas are crazy, or you have no money. But none of these things disqualifies you from serving Jesus! The only thing that can disqualify you is *unwillingness*.

When the great missionary Hudson Taylor was first called to serve the Lord in China, he was a young man with no training and little support. His fellow missionaries thought he was odd, but his faith in God and love for the Chinese people outshone all opposition and eventually resulted in thousands coming to Christ. Years later he wrote:

> God chose me because I was weak enough. God does not do His great works by large committees. He trains somebody to be quiet enough, and little enough, and then He uses *him*.[2]

God is drawn to weakness. When we realize that we can't do anything for him on our own, that's when he says, "Here's a person I can work through." When Jesus uses a weak person to do great things for his kingdom, he gets all the glory. So be encouraged. God is calling you!

Read | 1 Corinthians 1:26–31 and Hebrews 11:32–35

Reflect

1. According to the apostle Paul in 1 Corinthians 1:26–31, what kind of people does God call for his service? How might some of the words in this passage apply to you?

2. Why does God call people who are weak, lowly, and despised (see 1 Corinthians 1:28)? How does it glorify God when you depend on his strength?

3. Sometimes, we let past failures or life circumstances keep us from sharing Christ with others. But have you ever thought that your past difficulties might actually have *prepared* you to help others? What are some things you have experienced that could be a stepping stone for you to help people who are going through the same things?

4. How do you think God could take what you consider weaknesses and turn them into strengths, just like he did with Hudson Taylor (see Hebrews 11:33–34)?

Pray | End your time in prayer. Ask God to strengthen your faith and give you the willingness and courage to step out in obedience to serve him.

DAY 2
WHAT IS YOUR ASSIGNMENT?

When Jesus sent out the seventy, he instructed them to go "two by two ahead of him to every town and place where he was about to go" (Luke 10:1). God has a job for you too! He wants to use you in his work of saving people and growing them to maturity in Christ.

Sometimes, you might be tempted to think that because you aren't a great speaker or singer or leader, you don't have much to offer. But God has deliberately designed every person with particular gifts and tendencies. He has called you—and every other follower of Jesus—to serve him in ways that are perfectly suited to you.

One woman in the Bible, Dorcas, served widows by sewing them clothes (see Acts 9:36). A man named Tertius helped the apostle Paul write his letters (see Romans 19:22). Several men in the early church distributed food to believers in need (see Acts 6:1–6). Epaphras wrestled in prayer for the members of a particular church (see Colossians 4:12). What about you? You could help in the children's ministry at your church so parents could take part in the service. You could minister to people in a local shelter. You could visit those who are shut in or lonely. You could reach out to refugees. You could serve as a receptionist or financial manager or parking attendant in your church. The possibilities are endless.

Of course . . . God doesn't necessarily want us to come up with our own ideas about how we can serve him. No, he has prepared and crafted each of us for a specific assignment. So, how do you know what your job is? Simple. Ask God. The Holy Spirit will speak to you, put opportunities in front of you, and burden your heart. As God begins to lead you in a direction, he will confirm his guidance in his Word and through godly counsel from mature believers. As you step into God's purpose for you, he will use you powerfully to change lives.

Read | James 1:5–7 and Romans 12:6–8

Reflect

1. Sometimes you might feel prompted in your heart regarding a particular ministry, but you're not always sure if it's God leading or your own idea. This is especially true if loved ones think you're headed in a wrong direction. According to James 1:5–7, what does God promise to provide when you need direction? What is required on your part?

2. In Romans 12:6, Paul says that "we have different gifts, according to the grace given to each of us." While all of us are called to the work of God's kingdom, we don't all serve in the same way. How has God uniquely called *you* to share his love with others?

3. God will often call you to serve people who are different from you—in looks, race, economic background, culture, living circumstances. How open are you to letting go of what is comfortable or familiar and following Christ into his will for you?

4. You might think that your part in God's work is insignificant, but that's not true. God is the one who chose your task, and your work is needed. "Whether large or small, each person's assignment serves to advance the divine mission."[3] How does this encourage you today?

Pray | End your time in prayer. Ask God to show you your work assignment—and keep on asking until you hear from him.

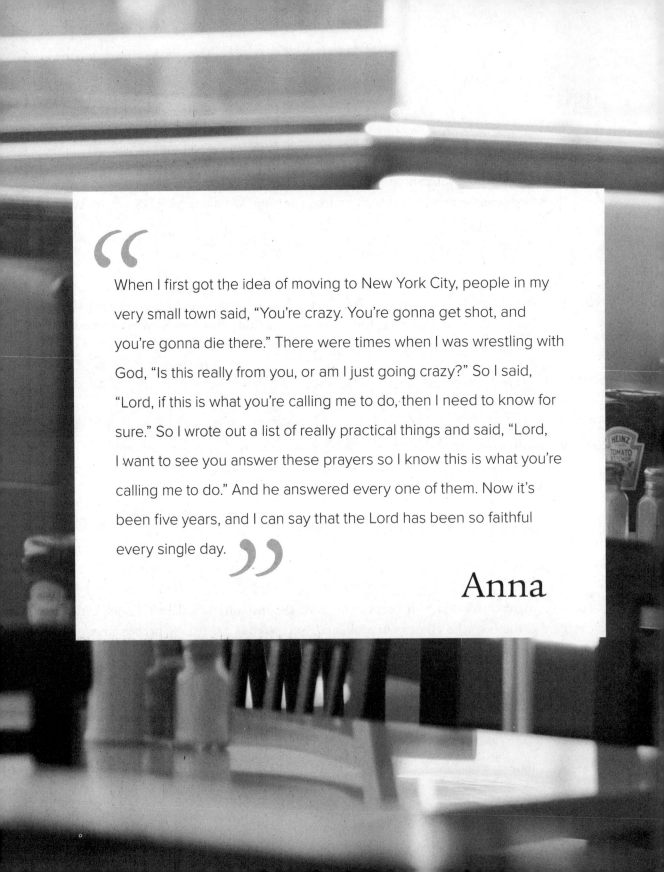

"

When I first got the idea of moving to New York City, people in my very small town said, "You're crazy. You're gonna get shot, and you're gonna die there." There were times when I was wrestling with God, "Is this really from you, or am I just going crazy?" So I said, "Lord, if this is what you're calling me to do, then I need to know for sure." So I wrote out a list of really practical things and said, "Lord, I want to see you answer these prayers so I know this is what you're calling me to do." And he answered every one of them. Now it's been five years, and I can say that the Lord has been so faithful every single day. "

Anna

DAY 3
OPEN YOUR EYES

Before Jesus sent out the seventy, he told them, "The harvest is plentiful." In another verse, he said something similar: "Open your eyes and look at the fields! They are ripe for harvest" (John 4:35). Jesus wasn't talking about a harvest of fruit and grain but of people! The Lord wants us to notice the men, women, and children around us—people who need the gospel.

We live in a busy world. We all have multiple demands on our time. But sometimes we can get so wrapped up in our own needs and responsibilities that we don't notice the people God brings across our paths—the lonely neighbor, the hurting family member, the overwhelmed young mother, the salesperson at our door, the hungry homeless person.

Jesus noticed people. You would think he would have gotten tired of them constantly following him and wanting his help. But Matthew 9:36 tells us that "when he saw the crowds, he had compassion on them, because they were harassed and helpless, like sheep without a shepherd." Jesus cared more about people's needs than about guarding his privacy. He saw their heartbreak and loneliness and spiritual need. The question is . . . do we?

As Lettie Cowman, author of the devotional *Streams in the Desert,* poignantly put it, "I expect to pass through this world but once. Any good work, therefore, any kindness, or any service I can render to any soul of man or animal, let me do it now. Let me not neglect or defer it, for I shall not pass this way again."[4] When the Lord calls us to take the gospel to others, he isn't making a light request. It is an urgent matter: "The harvest is plentiful! The fields are ripe! Open your eyes—people all around you are in need!"

The individuals God brings into our lives are often hiding great pain—but many of them are ready to receive the gospel. So let's ask the Lord to help us see people as Jesus does.

Read | Mark 6:30–34 and Acts 3:1–10

Reflect

1. When Jesus told the seventy that the harvest was plentiful, he was saying that people were ready to receive the gospel. How could knowing this make you more sensitive to the Holy Spirit's leading with each person the Lord brings across your path?

2. In Mark 6:30–34, the disciples had just returned from ministering the gospel, much in the same way that the seventy had done, and Jesus wanted to take them to a quiet place to rest. But when Jesus and his disciples arrived at their destination, they discovered they were not alone. How did Jesus handle this interruption of their plans? What did Jesus see in the crowds that we might have missed if we had been in his place?

3. Sometimes we are quick to notice the needs of people we feel close to but not so open to loving people who look different from us, or who frustrate us, or who hold views with which we disagree. How can you develop God's heart for people you would not naturally love on your own?

4. In Acts 3:1–10, when Peter and John went to worship at the temple in Jerusalem, they met a man who had been lame from birth asking for money. Instead of ignoring him, they "looked straight at him" (verse 4). They didn't consider this man an annoyance but a divine appointment. What do you think the Lord could do through you (and in you) if you saw people the same way that Peter and John saw that man?

Pray | End your time in prayer. Ask that the Lord will open your eyes to really see the people you come across and give you his heart for each one.

DAY 4

WHERE ARE ALL THE WORKERS?

When you think about how amazing it is that Jesus wants you to partner with him in building his kingdom, it would seem as if no believer would want to miss out. Yet when Jesus sent out the seventy to work in his harvest field, he made a sad statement: "The workers are few. Ask the Lord of the harvest, therefore, to send out workers into his harvest field" (Luke 10:2). The same is true in our day. *Where are all the workers?*

In America today, many Christians are content to just go to church once a week (if that). Some are more concerned with buying a new car, pursing a better job, or getting the latest iPhone than they are in fulfilling their assignment from God. But Jesus was clear when it came to addressing what our priorities should be:

> "So do not worry, saying, 'What shall we eat?' or 'What shall we drink?' or 'What shall we wear? . . . But seek first his kingdom and his righteousness, and all these things will be given to you as well" (Matthew 6:31, 33).

Jesus wants his church to be winning souls and making disciples. We find that after he told the seventy about the problem—"the workers are few"—he then told them what to do about it: "Ask the Lord of the harvest, therefore, to send out workers into his harvest field" (Luke 10:2). God is calling us to go—but he is also calling us to pray!

Prayer has to be the foundation of all God's work. As theologian and preacher A.B. Simpson wrote, "There is no ministry which will bring more power and blessing upon the world and from which we ourselves will reap larger harvests of eternal fruit than the habit of believing, definite, and persistent prayer for the progress of Christ's kingdom."[5] Yes, the workers are few, but if we bring the need to him in prayer, there's no telling what he will do to revive his church and raise up men and women to minister Christ to people who need him.

Read | Ephesians 6:18 and 2 Chronicles 7:14

Reflect

1. Consider the church in America today—not just your own church but God's people at large, as best you know. How do you think we are doing in taking the gospel of Christ to the men and women in our cities and neighborhoods and families? Why are there so few workers?

2. Remember what Jesus instructed the seventy to do about this problem—"Ask the Lord of the harvest . . . to send out workers into his harvest field" (Luke 10:2). What further insights does Paul provide in Ephesians 6:18 into how you can pray about this need?

3. What are some ministries or churches you could be praying for? List them below. Be sure to add your own church and pastor to the list! Perhaps you could commit to praying regularly for the leaders and workers in these groups—that the Lord would work powerfully through them as they send out workers into his harvest field.

4. In 2 Chronicles 7:14, we find several conditions and promises of prayer. If God's people were devoted to praying consistently and fervently that the Lord would send out workers into his harvest field, what do you think would happen?

Pray | End your time in prayer. Ask the Lord to awaken his church and to send out more and more workers for the building of his kingdom.

DAY 5
GOD WILL EQUIP YOU

Hopefully, God has stirred your heart this week about an assignment that he is calling you to do. But maybe you are still not sure if you can really step out to do what he's leading you to do. But remember—if Jesus is calling you to do a job for him, he will equip you for the task. God will never set you up for failure!

The seventy were not powerful or imposing figures. In fact, Jesus said that he was sending them out "like lambs among wolves" (Luke 10:3)! As they approached towns they had likely never visited before, walking in pairs, they probably asked one another, "Where should we start this time? What if these people don't like us?" Other than the basic instructions Jesus had given them, these servants had no idea what they were doing.

But Jesus opened doors and hearts that the seventy could never have opened on their own. We know this because when the seventy returned to Jesus after completing their mission, "They returned with joy and said, 'Lord, even the demons submit to us in your name'" (Luke 10:17). These brave individuals stepped out in faith, knowing nothing except that Jesus had saved them and sent them . . . and they saw the power of God change lives. Not only that, but their hearts were filled with joy in the process!

None of us has what it takes on our own to win people to Christ or effectively disciple believers. But when the Holy Spirit leads us into service for the Lord, he will work powerfully within us to draw people to himself and grow them to maturity. We will experience the joy of living out his purpose for our lives.

So trust God's leading. He will be with you as you step out in obedience and faith.

Read | Luke 21:13–15, Colossians 1:18, and 2 Chronicles 16:7–9

Reflect

1. Jesus told his disciples that when they testified about him, they were to make up their minds "not to worry beforehand" about what they would say because he would give

"

If you feel like the Holy Spirit is speaking to you, don't let fear or doubt get in the way of a blessing that God has for you and for others. If the Holy Spirit, who is the creator of the universe, is putting something on your heart, it's almost the same thing as when Moses had the burning-bush encounter. You may not be visually face to face with God, but he's speaking to you in your heart. When you act in obedience to what he's telling you, he will do exceedingly abundantly above anything you ask or think, because nothing's impossible for him. Don't think that because you don't have any initials behind your name or you're not an ordained minister that the Lord can't use you. All throughout the Bible, God uses his people, and we have him inside us to give us the power to do great things. "

Matt

them "words and wisdom" that no one could contradict (Luke 21:14–15). How would it help you to step out in faith if you made up your mind beforehand that you would not worry about the results but instead trust the Lord to speak and work through you?

2. According to Paul in Colossians 1:18, Jesus "is the head of the body, the church." As members of his body, how should you respond to Jesus' call? How can understanding that you need to obey the "head" help when you feel inadequate for the task?

3. According to 2 Chronicles 16:9, God is actually *looking* for people to help: "The eyes of the LORD range throughout the earth to strengthen those whose hearts are fully committed to him." What kind of people is God looking to strengthen? How does this verse speak particularly to you and your situation?

4. In what ways has the Holy Spirit spoken to you this week as you've thought about how God uses ordinary people? How have you been encouraged or challenged? How do you need God to guide, help, and empower you as you seek to step out in faith to serve Jesus?

Pray | End your time in prayer. Ask that God will fill you afresh with his Holy Spirit and equip you with all you need to do your work assignment for his kingdom.

SCHEDULE

WEEK 2

BEFORE GROUP MEETING	Read the Welcome section (page 25)
GROUP MEETING	Discuss the Connect questions Watch the video teaching for session 2 Discuss the questions that follow as a group Do the closing exercise and pray (pages 25–30)
PERSONAL STUDY – DAY 1	Complete the daily study (pages 32–33)
PERSONAL STUDY – DAY 2	Complete the daily study (pages 34–36)
PERSONAL STUDY – DAY 3	Complete the daily study (pages 37–38)
PERSONAL STUDY – DAY 4	Complete the daily study (pages 39–40)
PERSONAL STUDY – DAY 5 (before week 3 group meeting)	Complete the daily study (pages 41–43)

POWER FROM HEAVEN

*On one occasion, while he was eating with them, he gave them
this command: "Do not leave Jerusalem, but wait for the gift my Father
promised, which you have heard me speak about. For John baptized
with water, but in a few days you will be baptized with the Holy Spirit. . . .
You will receive power when the Holy Spirit comes on you;
and you will be my witnesses in Jerusalem, and in all Judea
and Samaria, and to the ends of the earth."*

ACTS 1:4–5, 8

Welcome | READ ON YOUR OWN

In the last session, we talked about seventy people in the Gospel of Luke whom Jesus sent out to pave the way before him. As we saw, these seventy individuals were not especially talented or dynamic. They were simply believers in Christ who made themselves available to him.

In the book of Acts, we find other stories of ordinary people who also made themselves available to God. Not only that, but we also see how the Lord powerfully equipped these people to do the work that he had called them to do when they chose to obey him. In this session, we are specifically going to look at the story of 120 believers who were empowered by the Holy Spirit to carry the flame of God's light and love to the world around them.

However, before these believers received this power, they first received some instructions from Jesus that to us might seem odd. When Christ was about to leave the earth, he basically said, "Don't go out and tell people I'm alive. Instead, wait in Jerusalem for the Holy Spirit to come on you." The world was lying in darkness, in need of the gospel, and Jesus said, "I want you to be my witnesses, but you can't do it effectively until you receive power from on high. The Holy Spirit will give you power, and *then* you will be my witnesses."

The church of Jesus Christ can only be built by supernatural power—when the flame of the Holy Spirit dwells in his people and they carry that flame to others. This is the history of the book of Acts. It is the history of the Christian church. Yes, we need to be available. But before we go out to serve, we—just like the 120 believers in the early church—need to be equipped by the Holy Spirit. Then we will be able to do our work assignments, not in our own power but in his.

Connect | 15 MINUTES

Take a few minutes to get better acquainted with your fellow members. Then choose one of the following questions to discuss as a group:

- What is something that spoke to your heart in last week's personal study that you would like to share with the group?

— *or* —

- When have you been eager to work on a project or carry out a plan—but you had to wait before you could start?

Watch | 20 MINUTES

Now watch the video for this session. Below is an outline of the key points covered during the teaching. Record any key concepts that stand out to you.

Outline

I. Every part of the body of Christ is to carry the flame. But where did the calling to carry the flame come from? In other words, how did the church begin?
   A. Jesus told his disciples to wait for the gift of the Father—the baptism of the Holy Spirit.
   B. People needed to hear the message of the gospel—yet Jesus told his followers to wait for power from heaven.
   C. We likewise need power from God in order to be bold witnesses for Christ.

II. The believers gathered in an upper room to wait for the fulfillment of this promise.
   A. On the Day of Pentecost, something came down from heaven (see Acts 2).
   B. This is the history of the church—God sending power from heaven to revive his people.
   C. Without the flame of the Holy Spirit, it is impossible for us to extend God's kingdom.

III. The early church, both apostles and lay people, went out in the power of the Holy Spirit.
   A. Ordinary believers were empowered so they could do their work assignment from heaven.
   B. When was the last time you asked God, "What is my work assignment?"

IV. The early church carried the flame by doing the work of the Lord.
   A. Every believer has a part to play. The work of the Lord is up to all of us.
   B. The work of the Lord is twofold: sharing the gospel and nurturing believers.

V. Paul wrote a personal message to one believer in the church in Colossae.
   A. Paul wrote to Archippus, "Complete the ministry you have received" (Colossians 4:17).
   B. Discouragement can stop us from doing the work we have been called to do.
   C. Stir up the flame, and then carry it. It's always too soon to quit.

Notes

Discuss | 35 MINUTES

Take some time to discuss what you just watched by answering the following questions. There are some suggested questions below that will help you begin your discussion, but feel free to pick any of the additional questions as well as time allows.

Suggested Questions

1. Review Acts 1:1–9. As noted in this week's teaching, when someone is about to leave and never be seen again, that person won't talk about trivialities. What was Jesus' final command to his disciples? What did he say would happen when they obeyed him?

2. Read Romans 8:9 and Ephesians 5:18. Although every believer *has* the Holy Spirit, not every believer has received *power* from the Holy Spirit. What does it mean to "keep being filled" with the Holy Spirit? Why is that important for followers of Christ?

3. What were the 120 doing while they waited for the promise from the Father? When have you met with other believers to pray for the empowering of the Holy Spirit in your life or church? (Compare your prayer time to the prayer meeting of the 120.)

4. Read Acts 2:1–4. How did God fulfill his promise to empower his people? Why do you think God poured out his Spirit on all 120 people and not just the apostles?

Additional Questions

5. Review Acts 4:1–12. In this story, Peter and John were seized by the religious authorities and thrown into jail for preaching the gospel. What happened after they were brought before the rulers, elders, and teachers of the law and asked, "By what power or what name did you do this?" (verse 7). What did this enable them to do?

6. The work of the Lord is twofold. First, it's about spreading the gospel so people can hear about Jesus and believe in him. Second, it's about nurturing those who believe so they will grow strong in their faith. How is your church carrying out both aspects of this work of the Lord? What are some ways your church could improve?

7. Consider this statement from the teaching: "When was the last time you stopped and prayed, 'Lord, where is my work assignment?' The Lord is not short on power, but he has to work that power through people who will carry the flame." How would you respond to this question? How have you seen him exercise his power through you?

8. In the letter of Colossians, Paul called out Archippus, a member of the church, and said, "See to it that you complete the ministry you have received in the Lord" (4:17). How will *you* make sure that you finish the work that God has called you to do?

Respond | 10 MINUTES

Take a few moments to reflect on the fact that God wants you to be available not to just to *do a job* for his kingdom but also to be available for the *Holy* Spirit to work in your life. Review the outline for the video teaching and any notes you took as you consider this point. Use the following questions to write down your most significant takeaways from this session.

What spoke most to your heart from the video teaching?

What do you sense God is stirring you to do as a result?

How can you make yourself more available to the Holy Spirit?

Pray | 10 MINUTES

End your time by praying together. Ask God to continue to empower each person in the group to do the work that he has assigned to them. Pray that he would give each person a "second wind" that would energize them to do the work that he has set for them. Conclude by asking if anyone has prayer requests to share, and then write those requests in the space below so that you and your members can continue to pray about them in the week ahead.

Name	Request

PERSONAL STUDY

It is impossible to do the work of God's kingdom without the empowering of the Holy Spirit. The Lord is looking for people who are not only open and *available* to be led but who are also open and *willing* to be empowered by the Holy Spirit. This week, you will have the chance to look at a few passages of Scripture that reveal why you need this empowering and how can receive it from the Lord. As you work through the exercises, be sure to write down your responses to the questions, as you will be given a few minutes to share your insights at the start of the next session if you are doing this study with others.

DAY 1

WAIT FOR THE GIFT

When Jesus was about to return to heaven and leave his followers to carry on his work on the earth, he gave them a few final instructions. He told them not to leave Jerusalem but to wait for the gift his Father had promised. "In a few days," he said, "you will be baptized with the Holy Spirit" (Acts 1:5). This seems like an unusual method of sending out followers. Why the delay?

Perhaps the answer can be found in the fact that Jesus was not setting up his followers just to do a *job*. He was preparing them for something far bigger: the birth of the *church*. The church, which would be made up of every person who put his or her faith in Jesus Christ for salvation, would be God's means of reaching the world for Christ. When Jesus returned to heaven, he would pour out his Holy Spirit on the church, and all God's people would then go throughout the world in the Spirit's power to take the gospel to everyone.

Those of us who make up the church today need this same empowering that the believers in the early church received. It's true, of course, that every believer in Jesus has the Holy Spirit living inside him or her—otherwise, that person wouldn't be a believer (see Romans 8:9). However, it's also true that a person can be saved yet not living in the power of the Holy Spirit, as was true of the church in Laodicea (see Revelation 3:14–22).

The Bible reveals that you need *ongoing* fillings of the Spirit to effectively carry out God's work (see Acts 4:8, 31). So, before you step out to do the work that God has called you to do, first take some time to wait on him. On your own, you can do nothing to build the kingdom, but with help from heaven, God will work powerfully through you.

Read | Acts 1:4–8 and Revelation 3:14–20

Reflect

1. According to the passage in the book of Acts, what two things did Jesus say would happen when the Holy Spirit came upon his followers (see verse 8)? How do you see

these two things playing out in your own church? How do you see these things playing out in your life?

2. What is the difference between the Holy Spirit *living* in a believer and the Holy Spirit *empowering* a believer for service? List some scriptures to support your answer.

3. According to Revelation 3:15–18, what is some of the evidence that the believers in the church in Laodicea were not being empowered by the Holy Spirit?

4. How could waiting on God for a fresh outpouring of his Holy Spirit affect the work you are currently doing for him?

Pray | End your time in prayer. Ask the Lord to help you learn to wait on him for the fullness of his Holy Spirit, and then spend a few minutes actually waiting on him.

DAY 2

PRAYER AND FIRE

The book of Acts reveals that the disciples did what Jesus had told them to do: they waited in Jerusalem for the promise of the Holy Spirit to come. The interesting thing is *how* they waited. They didn't teach or preach. They had a prayer meeting!

It wasn't just the apostles who joined together constantly in prayer. About 120 believers, both men and women, gathered to pray. After about ten days, the promise was fulfilled: "Suddenly a sound like the blowing of a violent wind came from heaven and filled the whole house where they were sitting. . . . All of them were filled with the Holy Spirit and began to speak in other tongues as the Spirit enabled them" (Acts 2:2, 4).

Jesus made it clear that his church can be built only by supernatural power. So why do we try to do it through programs or education or trends? Those efforts never work. They always lead to manmade institutions devoid of the life of the Spirit. We need to go back to the beginning. Like the 120, we need to call on God and wait on him for fresh power from heaven. The problem, as revival preacher Harold Vaughan notes:

> Many Christians are disinterested in prayer because they do not know its power. But this is a far cry from what we find in the early church. . . . Every member of the early church was a prayer-meeting Christian. They waited. They wept. They worshiped. And they watched the fire fall! The lack of holy fire in churches today indicates our need to return to upper room praying.[6]

Throughout church history, when believers have gotten weary of seeing no fruit, they have gone back to waiting on God for a fresh outpouring of his Holy Spirit. This is what Paul told Timothy to do when Timothy's fire was running low (see 2 Timothy 1:6). This is called revival! Serving the Lord in our own steam will never build God's kingdom. We need what the early church needed: the flame of the Holy Spirit.

Read | Acts 1:12–14, Acts 2:1–4; 2 Timothy 1:6–7, and James 5:16–18

Reflect

1. The first church was born in a prayer meeting. If the early believers needed to wait in prayer for the fullness of the Holy Spirit, don't we need to do the same? How would you say the church is doing in this area? How are you doing personally? Explain.

2. If we're going to carry the flame of the gospel to this world, we must first *fan* the flame so burns brightly in our lives. What encouragement does Paul provide in this regard in 2 Timothy 1:6–7? What does the empowering of the Spirit enable us to do?

3. The Bible is clear that all believers should stay connected to God through prayer . . . and yet there are a lot of believers in Christ today who don't seek out this connection on a daily basis. How could an understanding of James 5:16–18 revolutionize a believer's prayer life?

4. Would you describe yourself as a "prayer-meeting" Christian like those in the early church? Why or why not? If not, what are some steps you can take to become one?

Pray | End your time in prayer. Ask the Lord to make you a prayer-meeting Christian and to revive you and your church for his glory.

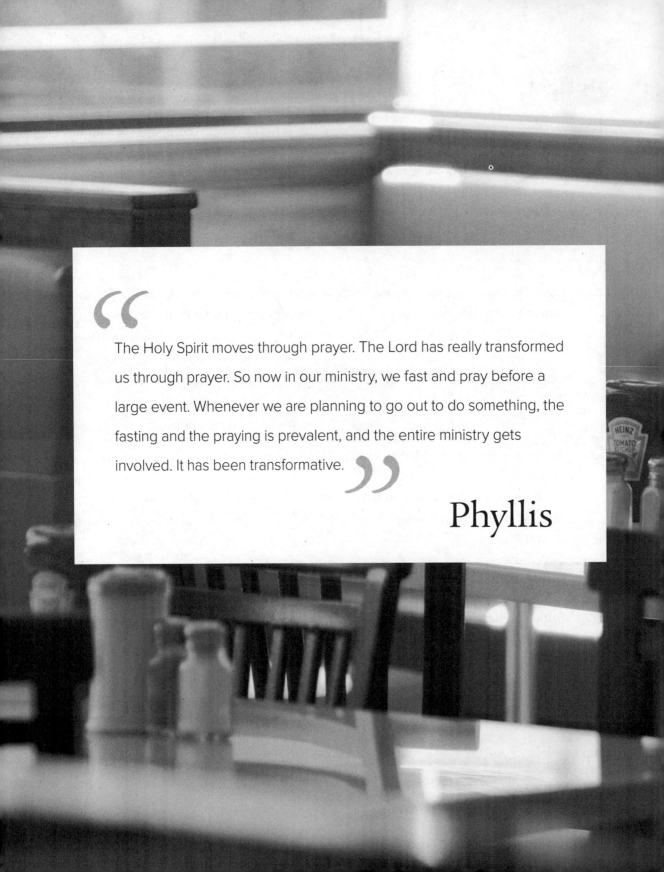

"

The Holy Spirit moves through prayer. The Lord has really transformed us through prayer. So now in our ministry, we fast and pray before a large event. Whenever we are planning to go out to do something, the fasting and the praying is prevalent, and the entire ministry gets involved. It has been transformative. "

Phyllis

DAY 3

SENT OUT IN POWER

When the Holy Spirit was poured out on the 120 believers, it changed *everything*. These believers were still ordinary men and women. But now they were filled, empowered, and sent out by the Holy Spirit to take the gospel to others.

Peter, an uneducated fisherman who had denied Jesus only a few weeks earlier, suddenly preached a bold sermon that cut people to the heart. Three thousand people were brought into the kingdom that day (see Acts 2:41). But God didn't pour out his Spirit just on the apostles. There were many lay believers who joined with the apostles with one heart and mind . . . and the Holy Spirit fell on each and every one of them.

When persecution later broke out against the early church, all the believers except the apostles scattered to the nearby regions. What did these lay Christians do when they were forced to leave their homes and found themselves in new areas without established churches? Did they wait for an apostle to come and lead them? Did they hide for fear of further persecution? No, they "preached the word wherever they went" (Acts 8:4).

Sadly, many Christians today, instead of going to church to serve, expect the leadership to carry out the work of ministry. They are more concerned with quickly getting out of the parking lot than they are with building God's kingdom. But Jesus did not save us so we can sit on the sidelines! Every single Christian is called to serve in God's kingdom.

God wants to empower you to carry out your assignment. It comes back to being available. You just need to say, "Lord, here I am! Send me! Fill me afresh with your Spirit!" When you are open in this way to the Holy Spirit, the Lord will do great things through you.

Read | Acts 2:14–41, Acts 8:1–4, and Romans 12:4–8

Reflect

1. Peter, who several weeks before had been afraid to admit that he even knew Jesus, now boldly "stood up" and "raised his voice and addressed the crowd" (Acts 2:14).

37

How did being filled with the Spirit change Peter's actions? How did it affect the people to whom he ministered (see verses 37, 41)?

2. In Acts 8:1–4, we see that "regular" Christians were just as bold and active in sharing their faith as the apostles were. What did these believers do when they were persecuted? How bold are you in sharing your faith? How does this passage challenge you?

3. In Romans 12:4–8, Paul lists several gifts that God has given to believers and encourages us to exercise our unique gifts. Which of the gifts in this passage apply most to you? How can you make yourself available to the Lord in this area of service to him?

4. When have you experienced church leadership and lay people serving together with one heart and mind? In what ways could this be done better in your church?

Pray | End your time in prayer. Thank the Lord that he has poured out his Spirit on all believers, including you! Then ask him to fill you and send you out to serve in his power.

DAY 4

THE WORK OF THE LORD

The fact that God wants us to carry the flame of his love to the world should motivate us to be eager to serve him. It should cause us to ask, "Lord, what is the assignment you have for me? Who are you calling me to serve?"

But sadly, we often allow God's call on our lives to take a back seat.

This was the problem among the members of the church in Corinth. They were excited about spiritual things, but they had allowed divisions to grow among them, and the work of the gospel was suffering as a result. So Paul wrote these instructions to them: "Stand firm. Let nothing move you. Always give yourselves fully to the work of the Lord, because you know that your labor in the Lord is not in vain" (1 Corinthians 15:58). "Hello!" he was saying. "Wake up! You need to be doing the work of the Lord."

What exactly *is* the work of the Lord? His work has two main goals: (1) to bring people to salvation in Jesus Christ, and (2) to help believers grow to maturity in Christ. In other words, *evangelism* and *discipleship*.

While every Christian sometimes does both, each of us is particularly gifted toward certain kinds of ministry. Some believers are called primarily to evangelism—winning souls for Christ. Others are called mainly to discipleship—teaching believers in the ways of the Lord so that even if their families turn against them, or they fail in some way, or they grow discouraged with life's problems, they will be strong in the Lord.

When Paul wrote to the Corinthian church, he wasn't writing just to the leaders. He was writing to the whole church. Who was to do the work of evangelism? Who was to nurture believers in Christ? *All* of God's people. So today, consider your work assignment from the Lord. Whatever it is—ministering to children, preaching on the street, praying for others, extending hospitality to others—don't be distracted or discouraged from it.

Keep at it! Don't quit! For as Paul said to the Corinthians, the work you do for Jesus Christ is not in vain.

Read | 1 Corinthians 15:58, Matthew 28:18–20, and 1 Corinthians 9:24–27

Reflect

1. What are the two main goals of the work of the Lord? Which of these areas do you believe you are the most called to perform? Explain your response.

2. When have you allowed the work of the Lord to take a back seat in your life? What have you done to get on track again?

3. In Matthew 28:18–20, we find Jesus instructing his disciples about the work they were to do for him after he went back to heaven. How do you see the two main aspects of the work of the Lord (evangelism and discipleship) in these words of Jesus?

4. Paul wrote in 1 Corinthians 9:24–27 that in our work for the Lord, we should "run in such a way as to get the prize." Which of the examples in this passage most encourages your heart? What will be the eternal results of doing the work of the Lord?

Pray | End your time in prayer. Ask the Lord to help you give yourself fully to his work and to remember that your work for him is not in vain.

DAY 5
TOO SOON TO QUIT

Being available to the Holy Spirit isn't a one-time thing. It involves yielding to God again and again . . . and pressing on in the assignment that he has given to us. Of course, this can be easier said than done! It's easy to get frustrated along the way and just want to give up.

Archippus, a believer in the early church, evidently had a problem in carrying out his ministry. The apostle Paul had never met this man, but somehow he had heard about his struggle. So Paul did something unusual. He wrote a letter to the church at Colosse—a church he had never visited—and challenged this particular Christian.

When the church received the letter, one of the believers read it aloud to the congregation. As he read about various topics—sound doctrine, freedom in Christ, holy living—he came to the final words of the letter that said, "Tell Archippus: 'See to it that you complete the ministry you have received in the Lord'" (Colossians 4:17).

Suddenly, everyone in the church was looking around to see where Archippus was. He was not a leader or an elder. He was just an ordinary man. Yet here Paul was, calling him out in front of the whole church.

Archippus had a calling from the Lord, but for some reason he hadn't stayed with it. He had gotten discouraged, or someone had criticized him, or his support system had been taken away, or he had tried something and failed—and Archippus had quit. Paul wrote to this one man and told him, "Don't quit! Finish the work God gave you to do!"

Just as God saw Archippus, he also sees you. He sees your fears and failings. He sees the opposition against you. But he also sees his calling on your life—and the reward he has for you at the other end. So, if the embers of your work assignment from the Lord are barely glowing, ask him to stir up the flame and help you carry that flame to others. Remember, the power to serve doesn't come from you but from heaven. If you persevere in your calling, at the end of the day, you will hear the Lord say, "Well done, good and faithful servant!"

Read | Galatians 6:9, Colossians 3:23, and Hebrews 12:1–3

Reflect

1. "Tell Archippus: 'See to it that you complete the ministry you have received from the Lord'" (Colossians 4:17). When have you been tempted to leave your work assignment from the Lord? How did you press through and overcome the temptation to quit?

2. Somewhere along the way, Archippus had grown weary of doing God's good work and was being tempted to quit in the ministry that he had received from the Lord. Perhaps you can relate. How do Paul's words in Galatians 6:9 encourage you to never give up in doing good for God? What promise are you given?

3. In Colossians 3:23, the apostle Paul tells us to work with all our hearts "for the Lord, not for human masters." When you do your work, who do you tend to serve—people or the Lord? How could trying to please people instead of Jesus affect your service for the Lord?

4. Hebrews 12:1–3 contains one of the most powerful pictures in Scripture of the eternal race we are running. How does this passage stir you to "throw off everything that hinders" and to "run with perseverance" the race marked out for you?

Pray | End your time in prayer. Ask the Lord to give you a fresh love for him and to help you complete the calling that you have received in him.

"

There were times I struggled. I cried. But I could not give up, because I wanted God to do something in my child's life. I had great faith that God could do something with her. He allowed her disability to happen for a purpose. I didn't understand what the purpose was until I came into God's Own, a ministry for children with disabilities where I served. There are times when you feel like you want to give up, but you can't give up. God doesn't give up on us, so I could not give up on what God wanted me to do. "

Myrna

SCHEDULE

WEEK 3

BEFORE GROUP MEETING	Read the Welcome section (page 47)
GROUP MEETING	Discuss the Connect questions Watch the video teaching for session 3 Discuss the questions that follow as a group Do the closing exercise and pray (pages 47–52)
PERSONAL STUDY – DAY 1	Complete the daily study (pages 54–55)
PERSONAL STUDY – DAY 2	Complete the daily study (pages 56–58)
PERSONAL STUDY – DAY 3	Complete the daily study (pages 59–60)
PERSONAL STUDY – DAY 4	Complete the daily study (pages 61–63)
PERSONAL STUDY – DAY 5 (before week 4 group meeting)	Complete the daily study (pages 64–65)

THE GIFT OF ENCOURAGEMENT

From time to time those who owned land or houses sold them, brought the money from the sales and put it at the apostles' feet, and it was distributed to anyone who had need. Joseph, a Levite from Cyprus, whom the apostles called Barnabas (which means "son of encouragement"), sold a field he owned and brought the money and put it at the apostles' feet.

ACTS 4:34–37

Welcome | READ ON YOUR OWN

In the previous session, we saw how the church was born when God poured out his Holy Spirit on 120 believers who were gathered together in an upper room in Jerusalem. Every believer—leader and lay person alike—was filled with the Spirit and empowered to take the gospel to the world. These believers formed a new community in which all "were one in heart and mind" and "shared everything they had" (Acts 4:32).

In this session, we are going to focus on one particular believer in the book of Acts who was generous with his resources and fulfilled a unique calling: encouraging other Christians. As we read, "Joseph, a Levite from Cyprus, whom the apostles called Barnabas (which means 'son of encouragement'), sold a field he owned and brought the money and put it at the apostles' feet" (verses 36–37). This man, Barnabas, was so filled with the Holy Spirit and the love of Christ that he couldn't seem to keep from helping other believers and lifting them up in the Lord.

When the flame of the gospel is burning brightly in a person or a church, people will likewise have a great love for others in need. Not only that, but they will also give sacrificially to help other people. This is a natural outflow of the Spirit of Jesus working in someone's life, because the Holy Spirit himself is an encourager, or comforter.

Encouragement is powerful . . . so powerful, in fact, that it can change a person's life. As we read in the book of Proverbs, "Gracious words are a honeycomb, sweet to the soul and healing to the bones" (16:24). Who among us hasn't been powerfully affected when someone has taken the time to reach out in our need, speak gracious words to us, and show us the love of Christ? When we make ourselves available to God by reaching out to people who need encouragement, we can do great things for his kingdom.

Connect | 15 MINUTES

Get the session started by choosing one of the following questions to discuss as a group:

- What is something that spoke to your heart in last week's personal study that you would like to share with the group?

— *or* —

- How has someone encouraged you in the last week or so?

Watch | 20 MINUTES

Now watch the video for this session. Below is an outline of the key points covered during the teaching. Record any key concepts that stand out to you.

Outline

I. The early believers sold their possessions to help people in need.
  A. When the flame of the Spirit is burning in a church, people care for those who are in need.
  B. Another sign of the flame burning brightly in a church is people giving sacrificially.
  C. No one told them to do this. It was a natural outflow of the Holy Spirit in them.

II. Joseph, a Levite from Cyprus, got a unique start in ministry.
  A. He sold a field and gave the money to the apostles, with no strings attached (see Acts 4:37).
  B. The church leaders saw how he encouraged others and changed his name to Barnabas.
  C. Do we not need that today in the Christian church with all the discouragement, all the negativity, all the nastiness, all the attacks on social media?

III. Encouragement is a gift of the Holy Spirit.
  A. Encouragement is not learned in seminary but is an overflow of the Spirit within us.
  B. Someone with the gift of encouragement refreshes others.
  C. God has encouraged you. You can encourage others!

IV. The ministry of encouragement can keep others going in their ministry for Christ.
  A. Often, all it takes is just a word or someone taking an interest in you to keep you going.
  B. It takes so little to be an encourager. It is something all of us could do.

V. Barnabas later went on to play a larger role in ministry.
  A. Promotion comes from the Lord. When we choose to encourage others, he will often move us into greater areas of impact for his kingdom.
  B. If you want to be great in God's kingdom, start by asking God to help you encourage someone in your life.
  C. Who knows where that prayer may lead? Who knows whose life you may change when you carry the flame of Jesus' encouragement? Let's carry that flame.

Notes

Discuss | 35 MINUTES

Take some time to discuss what you just watched by answering the following questions. There are some suggested questions below that will help you begin your discussion, but feel free to pick any of the additional questions as well as time allows.

Suggested Questions

1. Review Acts 4:34–37. In what unique way did Barnabas's ministry begin? How could you likewise start serving in simple ways by noticing obvious needs around you?

2. How did Barnabas get his nickname, and what does the name mean (see Acts 4:36)? If people were watching your lifestyle, what nickname would they give you?

3. There are two telltale signs of a church that is burning brightly with the flame of God's Spirit. First, the people have a great concern for those in need. Second, the people give sacrificially to help others. When have you seen a believer or a church overflowing with these two characteristics? What was the impact and the result?

4. In Romans 12:8, the apostle Paul says that encouragement is one of the gifts of the Spirit. Who do you know in your life who seems to have this particular gift? How has that person ministered to your life and affected where you are today?

Additional Questions

5. Who do you know who could use some encouragement? What practical things could you do to refresh the heart of that person or group of people?

6. We all know people who have the "gift" of discouragement. Maybe sometimes we are one of them! How can you bring the opposite quality of encouragement to people in your family? Your church? Your work? Your neighborhood?

7. In the teaching, Pastor Cymbala noted, "I know without a shadow of a doubt, I would not be sitting here today talking about carrying the flame if it wasn't for a son of encouragement who spoke into my life." How does this inspire you to step out of your routine, reach out, and encourage someone whom God has laid on your heart?

8. Barnabas started out by simply loving others and caring for them in practical ways. Later, he would go on to serve as a missionary alongside the apostle Paul. What qualities do you think God is looking for in the people he wants to promote?

Respond

Take a few moments to reflect on some of the ways that you, just like Barnabas in today's story from the book of Acts, can start to minister to others by encouraging them. Review the outline for the video teaching and any notes you took as you consider this point. Use the following questions to write down your most significant takeaways from this session.

What spoke most to your heart from the video teaching?

What do you sense God is stirring you to do as a result?

What will be your prayer this week as you seek to encourage others?

Pray

End your time by praying together. Ask the Holy Spirit to give you a heart of concern for those in need and a desire to sacrificially give of yourself to help them. Ask if anyone has prayer requests to share, and then write those requests in the space below so that you and your members can continue to pray about them in the week ahead.

Name   Request

PERSONAL STUDY

Encouragement, as you heard in this week's group time, is a gift of the Holy Spirit. But whether or not you *especially* have this gift, you can always be an encourager of other people! This week, you will have the chance to explore a few passages of Scripture to see what God says about how you can encourage the people in your life. As you work through these exercises, be sure to write down your responses to the questions, as you will be given a few minutes to share your insights at the start of the next session if you are doing this study with others.

DAY 1

SIGNS OF A BURNING FLAME

We all are called to serve the Lord in different ways. Some of us are called to feed the poor, some of us are called to teach children, and some of us are called to do administrative work. But in every person or church that is being led by the Holy Spirit, we will always find two qualities: (1) compassion for those in need, and (2) a willingness to give sacrificially to help meet the need.

When the first believers of the early church went out carrying the flame, it led to thousands placing their trust in Jesus as their Savior. As the church grew, an interesting practice developed: "those who owned land or houses sold them, brought the money from the sales and put it at the apostles' feet, and it was distributed to anyone who had need" (Acts 4:34–35). What a radical commitment to caring for each other!

The story then focuses in on one man: "Joseph, a Levite from Cyprus, whom the apostles called Barnabas (which means 'son of encouragement'), sold a field he owned and brought the money and put it at the apostles' feet" (Acts 4:36–37). Just imagine selling a piece of property and giving *all* the proceeds to the church to help others.

All too often, we miss the needs of our brothers and sisters in Christ. We go to church, say hello to people, and head back out into "real" life. But as we have seen, God wants us to notice people. What would happen if we slowed down and really saw the elderly woman sitting in front of us, the mom struggling with her children, the new couple who are shy and uncertain? Can't we give a few minutes to introduce ourselves, get to know someone a little, and be moved by their need? Maybe God is sending us to lift someone's heart and give that person the strength to keep going.

When we are filled with the Spirit of Jesus, no one has to tell us to encourage others. We will do it of our own volition, motivated by the flame of God's love in our hearts. So let's selflessly care for our brothers and sisters in Christ, like Barnabas did.

That's our real life.

Read | Acts 4:32–37, 2 Corinthians 9:6–8, and 1 John 3:16–18

Reflect

1. Who has encouraged you more than anyone else? What qualities does that person have that make him or her an encourager?

2. Paul wrote in 2 Corinthians 9:6 that "whoever sows sparingly will also reap sparingly, and whoever sows generously will also reap generously." In what ways will encouraging someone else bless you as well?

3. How did Jesus set the most perfect example of caring for others' needs? How are we to care for others in light of what he did for us (see 1 John 3:16)?

4. Consider the apostle John's words in 1 John 3:18: "Dear children, let us not love with words or speech but with actions and in truth." Who can you love today with actions and in truth? Write their names below, and then determine to reach out and encourage each one sometime during this week.

Pray | End your time in prayer. Thank the Lord for what Jesus has done to meet your need for salvation and ask him to help you love others as much as he loves you.

DAY 2

THE PLACE TO START

Maybe the Lord has put an idea for serving him in your heart, but you're not sure how to get started. You don't know the right people, or you're afraid of rejection, or you don't know if you've really heard from God. But you can always start serving the Lord the way Barnabas did: by encouraging other people.

As we have seen, Barnabas was not a leader in the church. He was just a man who saw a need in the community and thought, *If I sold my field, I could help a lot of people.* The apostles must have been watching him, because they changed his name. His real name was Joseph, but the apostles changed it to Barnabas, which means "son of encouragement." Given this, it is likely that selling his field and giving the money to the apostles was not his first act of helping others. Sharing with others must have been a lifestyle for him.

A person who stands out as an encourager shines as a bright light in this world. Every day, we come across so much negativity on social media, on the streets, in our homes. A simple word or act of encouragement can touch someone's heart deeply. So, if you're not sure how to carry the flame, a place to start is to do what Barnabas did: notice a need and do something about it. Start a conversation with someone you see sitting alone at church. Tell someone how much you appreciate what he or she has done. Ask someone how you can pray for him or her. This can be a simple and easy way to begin doing the work of the Lord.

Read | Philippians 2:1–4 and 1 Thessalonians 5:11

Reflect

1. How could encouraging someone be a first step toward doing whatever work assignment the Lord has laid on your heart?

2. In Philippians 2:1–4, Paul tells us that if we have been encouraged in Christ, then certain attitudes and behaviors should flow from us toward others. What are these qualities? What would a church that exhibited these qualities be like?

3. Paul writes, "Do nothing out of selfish ambition or vain conceit" (verse 3). The church leaders noticed that Barnabas was living a lifestyle of encouraging others—of sacrificial love for others. How could you likewise make encouraging others a lifestyle?

4. Paul wrote that we should "encourage one another and build each other up" (1 Thessalonians 5:11). How does encouraging others help strengthen the body of Christ?

Pray | End your time in prayer. Ask the Lord to revive your heart and help you step out in his love to meet someone else's needs.

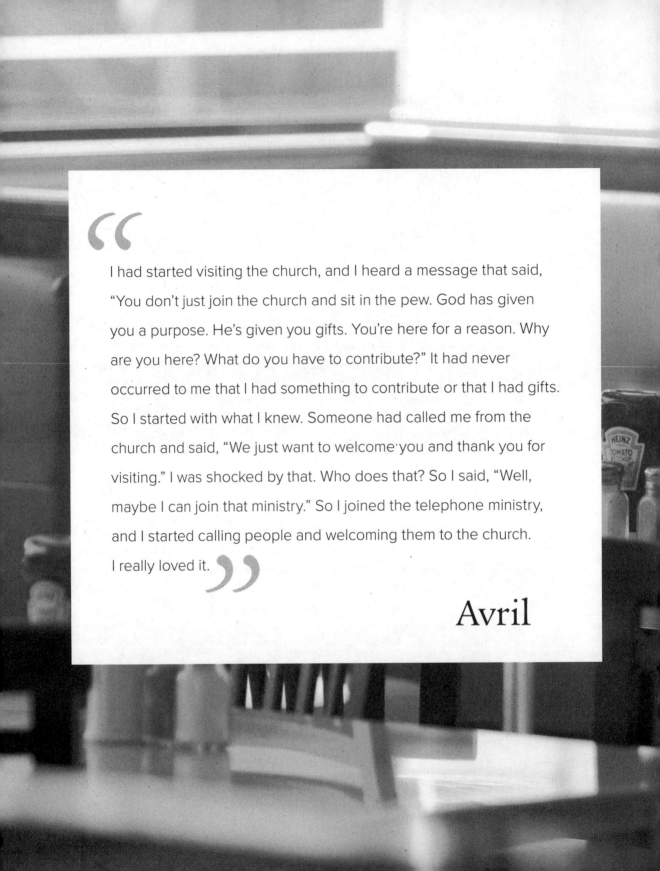

"

I had started visiting the church, and I heard a message that said, "You don't just join the church and sit in the pew. God has given you a purpose. He's given you gifts. You're here for a reason. Why are you here? What do you have to contribute?" It had never occurred to me that I had something to contribute or that I had gifts. So I started with what I knew. Someone had called me from the church and said, "We just want to welcome you and thank you for visiting." I was shocked by that. Who does that? So I said, "Well, maybe I can join that ministry." So I joined the telephone ministry, and I started calling people and welcoming them to the church. I really loved it. "

Avril

DAY 3
YOU CAN DO IT!

It doesn't take a seminary degree to be an encourager. Each of us can come alongside someone who is ready to quit and help him or her keep going. Sometimes, though, we get so buried in our problems that we don't think we can encourage anyone else. We get focused on ourselves and our needs, and the last thing we want to do is lift up other people.

But wait. Hasn't God encouraged you?

The word *encouragement* in Acts 4:36 comes from the same root word used to describe the Holy Spirit (see John 14:16).[7] The Spirit of Jesus is an encourager! He comes alongside us to lift us up. If we are filled with the Holy Spirit, then his love and concern for others will naturally flow out from our lives.

None of us needs to be down in the dumps! We have a choice. Even when we are in the hardest circumstances, we can wait on God and ask him for a fresh filling of his Spirit, and he will encourage us so that we can encourage someone else. That's what Paul means in 2 Corinthians 1:4 when he says that God "comforts us in all our troubles, so that we can comfort those in any trouble with the comfort we ourselves receive from God."

How refreshing it is to meet someone who says, "You can make it. It's too soon to quit! Come on, let me pray for you. Let's go out and have coffee. I want to tell you about the promises of God." So let's shake off discouragement and allow the Lord to fill us afresh with his strength and encouragement! We don't learn to encourage people by going to Bible school, being ordained, or becoming a pastor. No, any believer who is carrying the flame of God's love will naturally want to encourage other people.

Read | John 14:16–17, 1 Samuel 30:3–6, and 2 Corinthians 1:3–7

Reflect

1. Jesus said to his disciples, "I will ask the Father, and he will give you another advocate to help you and be with you forever" (John 14:16). The word for *advocate* can also be

translated as *helper* (NASB), *comforter* (KJV), and *counselor* (CSB). How has the Holy Spirit performed all these roles for you in times when you needed strengthening?

2. Moments of discouragement come to all of us, but we don't have to live in them. When David faced a tragedy, how did he recover from his grief and distress so that he could get back to helping others (see 1 Samuel 30:6)? How can you do the same?

3. In 2 Corinthians 1:8–11, Paul relates some of the difficulties he faced in Asia. However, God had delivered him from that trial, and he was confident the Lord would continue to deliver him in the future. What does Paul say in verses 3–7 about how God uses such difficulties to make us better encouragers and comforters to others?

4. What is one creative way that you can reach out to someone in need this week and offer some encouragement? What impact do you think this simple act on your part would have on that person's life?

Pray | End your time in prayer. Thank the Lord that he has sent his Spirit to encourage you and ask him to make you a glad encourager of others.

DAY 4

ENCOURAGEMENT CHANGES LIVES

Encouragement is powerful. It's so powerful, in fact, that it can change the course of a person's life. In the teaching for this week, Pastor Cymbala shared that one of the reasons he is in the ministry today is because someone encouraged him. "I wasn't really a strong Christian," he said. "I wasn't reading the Bible that much. But this man, an associate pastor, would always say, 'Come on, let's talk. Let's go to a restaurant, have coffee. Hey, Jim, I want you to read this version of the Bible.' And he would talk to me and encourage me."

This pastor then began to say, "You know what? Someday God is going to use you. God has a plan for you and your girlfriend, Carol. Just stay close to Jesus. Come on, you can do this." No one today knows this man's name. He never became famous. But because he followed the Holy Spirit's prompting to reach out to a young college basketball player, the Lord has ministered to many thousands of people through the ministry of Brooklyn Tabernacle.

We saw earlier how Barnabas sold his field to help other believers. But he also helped the apostle Paul get started in his ministry. The first time Paul went to Jerusalem after being saved, he tried to join the disciples, but they were afraid of him because of his violent past toward the church. But Barnabas stepped in and brought Paul to the apostles. He explained that Paul had met the risen Christ and had "preached fearlessly in the name of Jesus" (Acts 9:27). This opened the door for Paul to move freely in Jerusalem and preach the gospel.

What little it takes to be an encourager . . . but what a profound impact it can make on a life. So look for ways to reach out to someone in your world today. Your effort might seem small to you, but you never know what effect it will have on the kingdom of God.

Read | Acts 9:19–28 and Hebrews 10:24–25

Reflect

1. After Paul's conversion, he "spent several days with the disciples in Damascus" and "at once he began to preach in the synagogues that Jesus is the Son of God" (Acts 9:19–20).

From there, he traveled to Jerusalem. How did the believers in that city react when Paul attempted to join the disciples? What impact did Barnabas have on the situation when he stepped in and advocated for Paul (see Acts 9:26–28)?

2. The author of Hebrews encourages us to "consider how we may spur one another on" especially as the Lord's return draws near (Hebrews 10:24). How does this show the importance of reaching out to people when the Holy Spirit lays them on our hearts?

3. The author goes on to warn us not to "[give] up meeting together, as some are in the habit of doing, but [encourage] one another" (Hebrews 10:25). How does meeting regularly with other believers make it easier for us to encourage one another?

4. Who are some of the more unlikely people whom God might want you to encourage? Remember that while some of them might not seem to you to be good candidates for God to use, only the Lord knows the purposes that he has for each individual. What small acts can you take today to encourage that person in his or her faith?

Pray | End your time in prayer. Ask the Lord to help you understand what the people around you are going through so that you can speak to them a word in season.

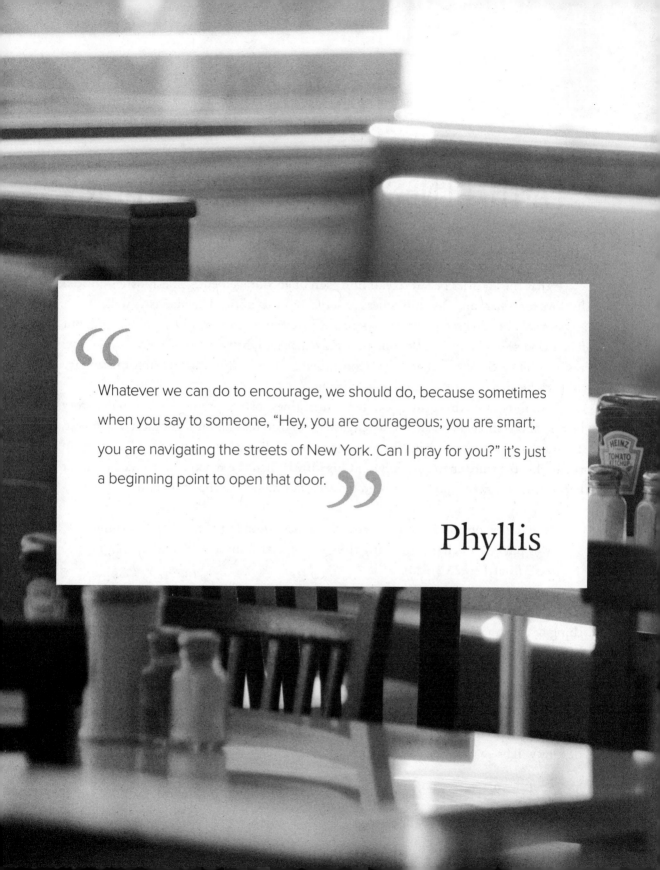

"Whatever we can do to encourage, we should do, because sometimes when you say to someone, "Hey, you are courageous; you are smart; you are navigating the streets of New York. Can I pray for you?" it's just a beginning point to open that door."

Phyllis

DAY 5

FAITHFULNESS BRINGS PROMOTION

Barnabas started out as a humble encourager. As we noted, he was so faithful at it that the apostles began to call him "son of encouragement." The apostles noticed his love for others and his willingness to serve. But *God* noticed Barnabas as well.

Barnabas hadn't set out to be noticed—he just wanted to be available to the Lord. But when God sees a heart like the one that Barnabas had, he raises that person to greater responsibility. So it was that when God called Paul to set out on his first missionary journey, he also called Barnabas to go with him.

Jesus illustrated this principle of how faithfulness brings promotion through a story he told about three men whose master gave them different amounts of money to invest. Two of the men were wise with the money and multiplied what their master had given to them. But the third man (literally) hid his gifts. When the master returned, he wasn't happy with the man who had refused to serve, but he said to the other two:

"Well done, good and faithful servant! You have been faithful with a few things; I will put you in charge of many things. Come and share your master's happiness!" (Matthew 25:21, 23).

God is looking for people who are available to the Holy Spirit and faithful in any little thing he asks them to do. So when he sees you doing the little things that you can do to lift up someone else, he will notice and call you to greater responsibility.

Maybe you want to be a pastor or a missionary or a ministry leader. Those are good desires. But start out by praying, "Lord, make me an encouragement to somebody today." Right now, today, make yourself available to God—not to cross the seas and be a famous missionary—but to speak a word of encouragement right where you live. Who knows what destiny will be changed because of it?

Read | Acts 13:1–4 and Matthew 25:14–30

Reflect

1. Promotion in ministry doesn't come from ourselves or from other people but from the Lord. How do you see this at work in Barnabas's life (see Acts 13:2)?

2. In the story that Jesus told in in Matthew 25:14–30, what did the two faithful men do that made their master happy (see verses 16–17)? How could encouraging other people be like multiplying the gifts that God has given you?

3. When have you felt like your service to the Lord didn't amount to much? How can being faithful in something small end up having big results?

4. How has the Lord most spoken to your heart in this session through the story of Barnabas? How will knowing that the Lord has encouraged you make you more of an encourager of others than you have ever been before?

Pray | End your time in prayer. Ask the Lord to make you an encourager like Barnabas so that you can say, do, or pray something that will lift someone else up.

SCHEDULE

WEEK 4

BEFORE GROUP MEETING	Read the Welcome section (page 69)
GROUP MEETING	Discuss the Connect questions Watch the video teaching for session 4 Discuss the questions that follow as a group Do the closing exercise and pray (pages 69–74)
PERSONAL STUDY – DAY 1	Complete the daily study (pages 76–77)
PERSONAL STUDY – DAY 2	Complete the daily study (pages 78–80)
PERSONAL STUDY – DAY 3	Complete the daily study (pages 81–82)
PERSONAL STUDY – DAY 4	Complete the daily study (pages 83–85)
PERSONAL STUDY – DAY 5 (before week 5 group meeting)	Complete the daily study (pages 86–87)

KEEP ON BEING FILLED

Be very careful, then, how you live—not as unwise but as wise, making the most of every opportunity, because the days are evil. Therefore do not be foolish, but understand what the Lord's will is. Do not get drunk on wine, which leads to debauchery. Instead, be filled with the Spirit, speaking to one another with psalms, hymns, and songs from the Spirit.

EPHESIANS 5:15–19

Welcome | READ ON YOUR OWN

In this study, we have looked at how ordinary believers in the New Testament were filled with the flame of the Holy Spirit and did extraordinary things for God. The seventy followers of Jesus made themselves available to him and paved the way for the spread of the gospel (see Luke 10:1–24). The 120 believers waited in an upper room and prayed, and the Holy Spirit fell on them (see Acts 1:12–15; 2:4). Barnabas, filled with the Holy Spirit, encouraged so many that he was nicknamed "son of encouragement" (see Acts 4:36–37).

We have been talking about *carrying the flame*—the flame of the gospel . . . the flame of the light and love of Christ. But most often in the New Testament, the flame (or fire) refers to the person of the Holy Spirit and his work in the life of a believer and in a church:

> When the day of Pentecost came, they were all together in one place. Suddenly a sound like the blowing of a violent wind came from heaven and filled the whole house where they were sitting. They saw what seemed to be *tongues of fire* that separated and came to rest on each of them (Acts 2:1–3, emphasis added).

When we carry the flame, we are carrying within us the Holy Spirit, who touches others through us with his light and love and truth. This is what we will examine in this session . . . what it means to carry the flame and be filled with the Spirit.

In particular, we will look at *who* the Holy Spirit is and *what* he is about. Jesus said, "When he, the Spirit of truth, comes, he will guide you into all the truth" (John 16:13). The Holy Spirit guides us and reveals the truth of God to us. So, it's important for us to know who the Holy Spirit is so we can align with his purposes in our lives.

Connect | 15 MINUTES

Get the session started by choosing one of the following questions to discuss as a group:

- What is something that spoke to your heart in last week's personal study that you would like to share with the group?

— or —

- What is one thing you know about the Holy Spirit?

Watch | 20 MINUTES

Now watch the video for this session. Below is an outline of the key points covered during the teaching. Record any key concepts that stand out to you.

Outline

I. Jesus told his disciples, "It is for your good that I am going away. Unless I go away, the Advocate will not come" (John 16:7). He also said to them, "I have been *with* you, but the Holy Spirit will be *in* you."

    A. Jesus' verbal teaching didn't change the disciples all that much—on the night that Christ was betrayed, they all fled (see Mark 14:50).

    B. The Holy Spirit would be inside Jesus' followers, living through them from the inside out.

II. The Holy Spirit is often neglected in the church today.

    A. Some Christians lean toward unbiblical fanaticism regarding the Holy Spirit.

    B. Other Christians, reacting to this fanaticism, pull back from the Holy Spirit altogether.

III. Every believer has the Holy Spirit inside of him or her (see Romans 8:9), but not all believers have the power of the Holy Spirit.

    A. We want to not only be Bible-filled but also Spirit-filled believers.

    B. This is why Paul told us to *keep on* being filled (see Ephesians 5:18).

IV. The work of God can be done only by those filled with his Holy Spirit.

    A. The book of Acts is about the acts of the Holy Spirit as he worked through—apostles, yes—but also ordinary people like you and me.

    B. God can use anyone who is available to him and filled with his Spirit.

    C. Unless God helps us, we can't do anything for him.

V. The Holy Spirit is God on earth.

    A. The Holy Spirit comes to glorify Christ (see John 16:14).

    B. We must not grieve or quench the Holy Spirit (see Ephesians 4:30; 1 Thessalonians 5:19).

    C. We must not resist him (see Acts 7:51) but yield ourselves totally to him.

Notes

Discuss | 35 MINUTES

Take some time to discuss what you just watched by answering the following questions. There are some suggested questions below that will help you begin your discussion, but feel free to pick any of the additional questions as well as time allows.

Suggested Questions

1. Why did Jesus tell his disciples that it would be good for them if he went away (see John 16:7)? Why was it hard for them to understand what he was saying?

2. According to the teaching, the Holy Spirit is often neglected in the church today. What unbiblical excesses in the name of the Holy Spirit have you seen that could cause Christians to distance themselves from, or neglect, the true working of the Spirit?

3. Consider this statement: "Every believer has the Holy Spirit in him. . . . But it is obvious from the New Testament and church history that not all Christians have that power imparted to them." Why is it so critical that we receive this empowering of the Holy Spirit? What happens in churches were his power is absent?

4. Paul instructs, "Do not grieve the Holy Spirit of God" (Ephesians 4:30). What are some things that grieve the Holy Spirit? When have you seen this happen?

Additional Questions

5. We see in the Gospels that Jesus' verbal teaching did not necessarily lead to transformation in his disciples. On the night Jesus was betrayed, Peter three times denied knowing him, and "all the disciples deserted him and fled" (Matthew 26:56). How is it possible for believers in Christ to read God's words (the Bible) but not be changed? Although knowing Scripture is vital, what actually brings about change in us?

6. When the great evangelist D.L. Moody was asked, "Why do you keep emphasizing being filled with the Holy Spirit over and over again?" he replied, "Because I leak." What do you think he meant by this statement? What was he implying that he needed?

7. Today, we refer to the book of Acts as the "Acts of the Apostles," but that title was actually added to it around the end of the second century AD. What is the book of Acts *really* about? In other words, whose "acts" are seen in it? What evidence can you provide of who the book is about based on stories from Acts that you know?

8. How can our weaknesses and deficiencies help us lean more on the Holy Spirit?

Respond | 10 MINUTES

Take a few moments to reflect on the fact that you must be *continually* filled with the Holy Spirit to accomplish God's purposes on this earth. Without this power, you can do nothing effectively for God. Review the outline for the video teaching and any notes you took. Use the following questions to write down your most significant takeaways from this session.

What spoke most to your heart from the video teaching?

What do you sense God is stirring you to do as a result?

What will you do this week to be continually filled with the Holy Spirit?

Pray

End your time by praying together. Ask the Lord to continually fill you with his Spirit as you head into this next week and commit to being completely open to his leading in your life. Ask if anyone has prayer requests to share, and then write those requests in the space below so that you and your members can continue to pray about them in the week ahead.

Name   Request

PERSONAL STUDY

*C*arrying the flame, as you discussed in this week's group time, requires us to be filled with the Holy Spirit. But who is the Holy Spirit? What does he do? This week, you will explore a few passages of Scripture that reveal what it means to be filled with the Holy Spirit on an ongoing basis and how that affects your service for him. As you work through these exercises, be sure to write down your responses to the questions, as you will be given a few minutes to share your insights at the start of the next session if you are doing this study with others.

DAY 1

FOR OUR OWN GOOD

If anyone was the perfect teacher, it was Jesus. If anyone should have experienced transformation as a result of that teaching, it was the disciples. But after three years of instruction, the Gospels reveal that the disciples remained mostly unchanged. They still gave way to fear, hardened their hearts, rejected people they should have loved, and argued about whom among them was the greatest. At Jesus' arrest, they ran for their lives, and Peter even denied knowing him.

When Jesus told his disciples that he would be leaving them, they were none to happy at the news. But Jesus told them that his going would be for their good, because when he left, he would send the Holy Spirit. The Spirit would be not just *with* the disciples, as Jesus had been, but also *in* them (see John 13:33; 14:16–17; 16:7).

Jesus' verbal teaching was vital, of course. The disciples needed to hear it, and we do too. We should know the Word of God and be able to rightly divide it (see 2 Timothy 2:15). But knowledge of Scripture alone will never change a person. We need the Holy Spirit inside us to help us not just know the Word but also understand it, receive it, and live it out. As Methodist preacher Samuel Chadwick once said, "Christianity is hopeless without the Holy Spirit."[8]

Jesus' words were proven true when the Holy Spirit was poured out on the 120 believers who were gathered together in the upper room and they became powerful witnesses for Christ. Andrew Murray, a South African minister, said of this event, "He whom they had known in the flesh, living with them on earth, they now received by the Spirit in His heavenly glory within them. Instead of an outward Jesus near them, they now obtained the inward Jesus with them."[9]

When Jesus was on earth, he was in charge. When he left, he sent the Holy Spirit to be in charge. The disciples had looked to Jesus for guidance. Now, they needed to look to the Spirit, who would guide them "into all the truth" (John 16:13). We need to do the same.

Read | Luke 24:36–45, John 14:16–17, and John 16:7–13

Reflect

1. In Luke 24:36–45, Jesus appeared to his disciples after the resurrection and "opened their minds so they could understand the Scriptures" (verse 45). What did Jesus remind them had been written about him? Why do you think the words that Jesus said to them about his death and resurrection didn't "take" until they witnessed it?

2. Andrew Murray noted, "Instead of an outward Jesus near them, they now obtained the inward Jesus with them." How does this shed light on who the Holy Spirit is?

3. If the Holy Spirit is the Spirit of Jesus himself, why do you think there is often little teaching on the Holy Spirit in the church—and sometimes even an avoidance of him?

4. Why is Christianity, as Samuel Chadwick said, hopeless without the Holy Spirit?

Pray | End your time in prayer. Thank the Lord for sending his Holy Spirit and ask him to help you understand more and more who his Spirit is.

DAY 2
BIBLE FILLED AND SPIRIT FILLED

If the Holy Spirit is in charge of the church, it goes without saying that we need to know who he is. Unfortunately, as we have discussed, the Holy Spirit is often neglected in the church today. Why is this?

One explanation is that some churches fear that talking about the Holy Spirit could lead to an out-of-balance focus on him . . . which in turn could lead to fanaticism and behavior that contradicts Scripture. So, in an attempt to honor the Word of God, they refrain from even discussing him. But in the process, they also avoid *emphasizing* the importance of the Holy Spirit in a believer's life. They focus on Bible study, and may talk about the fruit of the Spirit—love, joy, peace—but they avoid certain expressions of the Spirit's power.

Most Christians believe in the fullness of the Holy Spirit, but as theologian A.W. Tozer wrote, "Nobody experiences it . . . it lies under the snow, forgotten."[10] Why is this? Tozer continues: "I believe it has been the work of the devil to surround the person of the Holy Spirit with an aura of . . . strangeness, so that the people of God feel that this Spirit-filled life is a life of being odd and peculiar, of being a bit uncanny. That is not true, my friend! . . . [The Holy Spirit] is only the essence of Jesus imparted to believers."[11]

We should be Bible filled, but we should also be Spirit filled. After all, it's the Holy Spirit who makes the Word of God come alive to our hearts. Without his illuminating power within us, the Word will only touch our minds. Instead, balanced Christianity honors the Bible *alongside* a childlike dependence on and openness to the Holy Spirit.

Read | John 5:39–40 and 1 Corinthians 14:26–33

Reflect

1. According to Tozer, "It has been the work of the devil to surround the person of the Holy Spirit with an aura of . . . strangeness, so that the people of God feel that this Spirit-filled life is a life of being odd and peculiar." When have you seen this attitude

in Christians? Why do you think it might be the devil's strategy to make the Holy Spirit seem odd and peculiar?

2. While we absolutely need the Word of God and correct doctrine, we also need to be open to the work of the Holy Spirit in our lives. According to John 5:39–40, how did the Pharisees know the Scriptures well yet at the same time resist the Lord?

3. While we need the fullness of the Holy Spirit, we also need to walk biblically and in order. According to 1 Corinthians 14:26–33, how did the believers in Corinth embrace the Holy Spirit yet need correction regarding the use of spiritual gifts?

4. Consider your own life. Would you say that you are more Bible filled or Spirit filled? Explain your response. How can you grow in both of these areas?

Pray | End your time in prayer. Thank the Lord for his Word and his Spirit, and ask him to make you both Bible filled and Spirit filled.

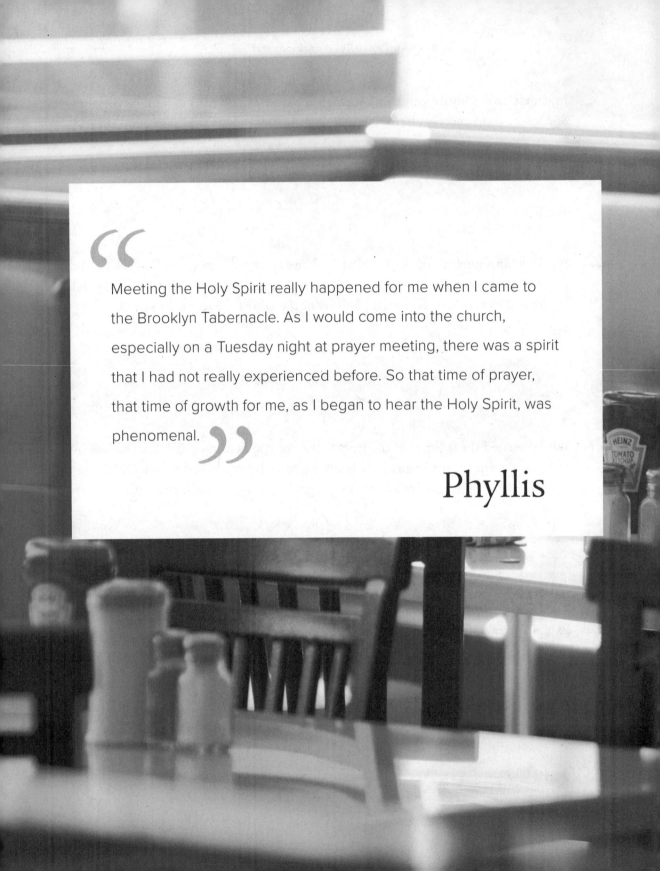

"Meeting the Holy Spirit really happened for me when I came to the Brooklyn Tabernacle. As I would come into the church, especially on a Tuesday night at prayer meeting, there was a spirit that I had not really experienced before. So that time of prayer, that time of growth for me, as I began to hear the Holy Spirit, was phenomenal."

Phyllis

DAY 3
A CONTINUAL FILLING

We've noted throughout this study that while every believer in Christ has received the *indwelling* of the Holy Spirit (see Romans 8:9), not every believer has received the *empowering* of the Holy Spirit. In the book of Revelation, we find Jesus telling the church in Laodicea, "Because you are lukewarm—neither hot nor cold—I am about to spit you out of my mouth" (Revelation 3:16). How could we possibly say that this church was filled with the Spirit of God?

Some Christians believe that when the Holy Spirit was poured out at Pentecost, it was just a one-time event. But even people who were filled with the Holy Spirit on that day were filled again. Peter, for example, was filled a second time when he was challenged by the religious leaders and spoke boldly to them in the name of Jesus (see Acts 4:8). We need to be filled with the Spirit again and again.

In Ephesians 5:18, the apostle Paul tells us to "be filled with the Spirit." In the original Greek, the term used for "be filled" indicates that we are to be continually filled, or keep on being filled.[12] Commentator David Guzik writes:

> Paul's grammar here clearly says, "be *constantly being filled* with the Holy Spirit." . . . The filling of the Holy Spirit is not a one-time event that we live off of the rest of our days. It is a constant filling, asking to be filled, and receiving the filling by faith.[13]

As noted in the group time, the evangelist D.L. Moody once said, "We are leaky vessels, and we have to keep ourselves under the fountain all the time in order to keep ourselves full of Christ, and so have a fresh supply of his power and his grace."[14] We keep ourselves "under the fountain" by spending time with the Lord. We need a fresh supply of the Holy Spirit in our lives each and every day so that we can face the challenges of life not in our own strength but in the power of the Spirit.

Read | Acts 4:1–13 and Luke 11:9–13

Reflect

1. Peter had been filled with the Holy Spirit on Pentecost, but in Acts 4:8, we read that he was again "filled with the Holy Spirit." Why do you think he needed a fresh filling? What are some situations you've faced recently where you needed a fresh filling of the Holy Spirit?

2. In Luke 11:9–13, Jesus speaks about the need for persistent prayer. "Ask and it will be given to you; seek and you will find; knock and the door will be opened to you" (verse 9). Ultimately, what was Jesus telling us to ask the Father to provide? How does this passage encourage you as you seek the ongoing filling of the Holy Spirit?

3. D.L. Moody wrote "that we have to keep ourselves under the fountain all the time in order to keep ourselves full of Christ." What are some ways that you can do this?

4. What are the traits of a person who is being continually filled with the Holy Spirit? What are the traits of a person who is *not* being continually filled in this manner?

Pray | End your time in prayer. Praise the Lord for his Holy Spirit and ask him to fill you afresh today in the circumstances you face.

DAY 4
ONLY BY THE SPIRIT

In an earlier session, we discussed how some of the early believers in the church sold property and gave the proceeds to help other Christians. As the church grew, the members also shared their food with each other (see Acts 4:32–37). This worked well . . . until the Greek Jews began to complain against the Hebrew Jews that their widows were being overlooked in the daily food distribution.

So, the apostles gathered everyone together and said, "Choose seven men from among you who are known to be full of the Spirit and wisdom. We will turn this responsibility over to them" (Acts 6:3). Even to hand out food, the church needed people who were full of the Holy Spirit. All the apostles' acts were the acts of the Holy Spirit working through them.

This was true for the rank-and-file believers as well. The 120 believers in Acts 2 had no special power; they just prayed and waited on God. Barnabas had no great strength; he just sold a field and encouraged others. Philip, whom we'll discuss in the next session, had no specials skills to speak of in evangelism; he just had a trusting and obedient heart. The common denominator in all these people is that they were *filled with the Spirit.*

The church will never grow as it should without men and women who are full of the Spirit of Jesus. The early believers didn't try to be relevant to their culture. They simply spent time with Jesus and were filled continually with his Spirit. Then they went out in his power, and people were saved and discipled. No matter what God asks us to do—loving children, working in an office, helping the poor, evangelizing on the street—we need to be full of the Holy Spirit.

Read | Acts 6:1–7, Philippians 4:12–13, and Hebrews 11:32–34

Reflect

1. "In those days when the number of disciples was increasing, the Hellenistic Jews among them complained against the Hebraic Jews because their widows were being

overlooked in the daily distribution of food" (Acts 6:1). Why do you think the twelve disciples instructed the Christian community to select seven men who were "known to be full of the Spirit" (verse 3) to to resolve this matter?

2. What does Paul say in Philippians 4:13 that we can do when the Lord strengthens us? What are some current obstacles in your life that can be overcome by this promise?

3. Based on Hebrews 11:32–34, what can God do in a person who, through faith, depends on the Holy Spirit? Which of the things in this passage most encourages you?

4. Consider this statement from this week's teaching: "You have no concept what God can do through your life if that flame touches you and you are sensitive and yielded to God's will and plan for your life." How will you, like the believers in the book of Acts, rise up in faith and see what acts the Holy Spirit wants to do through you?

Pray | End your time in prayer. Thank the Lord that in your weakness, he is strong.

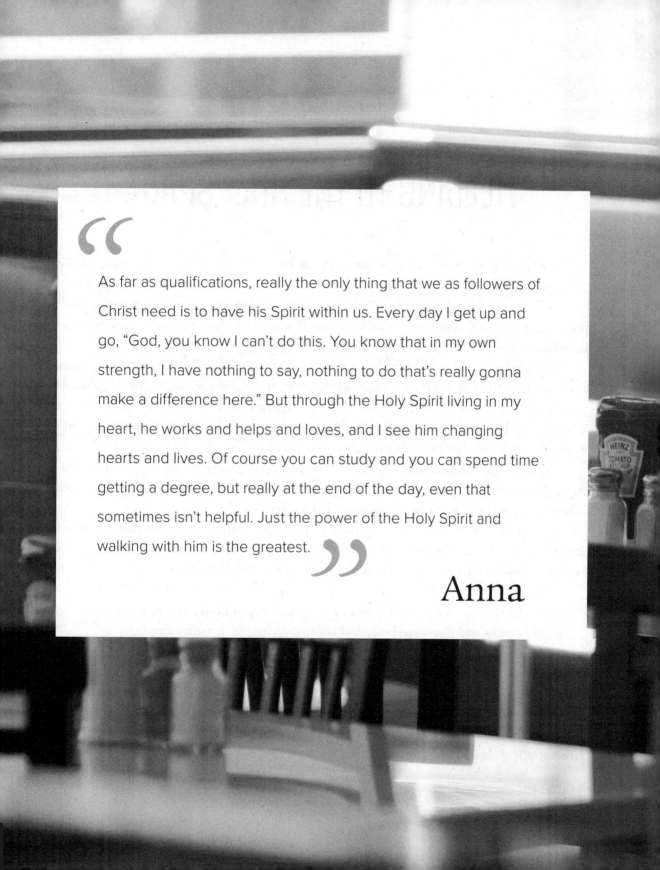

"

As far as qualifications, really the only thing that we as followers of Christ need is to have his Spirit within us. Every day I get up and go, "God, you know I can't do this. You know that in my own strength, I have nothing to say, nothing to do that's really gonna make a difference here." But through the Holy Spirit living in my heart, he works and helps and loves, and I see him changing hearts and lives. Of course you can study and you can spend time getting a degree, but really at the end of the day, even that sometimes isn't helpful. Just the power of the Holy Spirit and walking with him is the greatest.

"

Anna

DAY 5

YIELDING TO THE HOLY SPIRIT

The Holy Spirit is not an impersonal power or a force but a person. Unfortunately, according to one recent study, "[Many] self-identified born-again Christians contend that the Holy Spirit is not a real, living being but is merely a symbol of God's power, presence or purity."[15] However, the Bible is clear that the Holy Spirit is God . . . and because he is God, we should yield to him.

Often, however, we don't obey the Holy Spirit. Instead, we grieve him. We can actually make God sad! The Holy Spirit within us is like a gentle, delicate dove. As theologian and preacher A.B. Simpson stated, when we do not cooperate with the Holy Spirit's will, "His heart is vexed, His love is wounded, His purpose is baffled; and if the Comforter could weep, we would see the tears of loving sorrow upon His gentle face."[16]

We can also quench the Holy Spirit. This is like pouring water on a fire. We can do this through a lying, gossip, not loving others—anything we yield to that is not of the Lord. When we quench the Spirit, we cannot carry the flame.

Some of us even resist the Holy Spirit. This happens when we try to tell God our plans for serving him instead of submitting to him. But we can never fit the Holy Spirit into a box of our own making. E.M. Bounds, the great writer on prayer, once said:

> What the Church needs today is not more machinery or better, not new organizations or more and novel methods, but men whom the Holy Ghost can use.[17]

We either yield fully to the Spirit, which brings untold blessing, or we resist him and miss out on so many things that he has for us.

Are you lacking peace and joy? Could it be that you are grieving, quenching, or resisting the Spirit of God in some way? Let's not hold any part of our lives back from the Lord. Let's give ourselves wholly to him, no matter the cost.

Read | Ephesians 4:30, 1 Thessalonians 5:19, Acts 7:51, and Galatians 5:22–23

Reflect

1. We might think that God's first reaction to our sin would be judgment. How does it impact you to know that the Holy Spirit is actually grieved, or saddened, when we sin against him?

2. What are some ways we could grieve, quench, or resist the Holy Spirit? What are some ways we could bring joy to the Holy Spirit?

3. What kind of fruit does the Holy Spirit produce in a person who is yielding to him? Which of these qualities do you most desire to see increased in your life? Why?

4. What has the Lord most impressed on your heart through this session's study of the Holy Spirit? How will this impact your life and service for him?

Pray | End your time in prayer. Thank the Lord for his gentleness toward you, and ask him to help you yield to him, no matter the cost.

SCHEDULE

WEEK 5

BEFORE GROUP MEETING	Read the Welcome section (page 91)
GROUP MEETING	Discuss the Connect questions Watch the video teaching for session 5 Discuss the questions that follow as a group Do the closing exercise and pray (pages 91–96)
PERSONAL STUDY – DAY 1	Complete the daily study (pages 98–100)
PERSONAL STUDY – DAY 2	Complete the daily study (pages 101–102)
PERSONAL STUDY – DAY 3	Complete the daily study (pages 103–105)
PERSONAL STUDY – DAY 4	Complete the daily study (pages 106–107)
PERSONAL STUDY – DAY 5	Complete the daily study (pages 108–110)

THE HOLY SPIRIT STILL SPEAKS

The Spirit told Philip, "Go to that chariot and stay near it." Then Philip ran up to the chariot and heard the man reading Isaiah the prophet. "Do you understand what you are reading?" Philip asked. "How can I," he said, "unless someone explains it to me?" So he invited Philip to come up and sit with him. . . . Then Philip began with that very passage of Scripture and told him the good news about Jesus.

ACTS 8:29–35

Welcome | READ ON YOUR OWN

Throughout this study in *Carry the Flame*, we have seen how the Lord does great things through regular people who are surrendered to him and willing to be led by his Spirit. In this final session, we will look at one last account from the book of Acts—of a man named Philip. This individual was available to the Holy Spirit and used powerfully by the Lord to bring someone to know Christ.

The story begins when a great persecution breaks out against the church in Jerusalem and all the believers (except the apostles) scatter throughout Judea and Samaria. As we read, "Saul began to destroy the church. Going from house to house, he dragged off both men and women and put them in prison" (Acts 8:3). But as these believers flee, they carry the flame of the gospel with them, and revivals break out in city after city. Philip is taking part in this great revival when an angel of the Lord tells him to leave that place and travel to a barren desert road that leads from Jerusalem to Gaza.

Philip must have wondered what this was about . . . but he obeyed and went. When he got to the road, the Holy Spirit directed him to a man in a chariot. This led to a God-created conversation, and the man ended up being saved and baptized. Tradition tells us that he carried the gospel to his homeland and to thousands of others (see Acts 8:26–40).

The Holy Spirit spoke to Philip through the angel. But does he *still* speak today? This is the focus of this final session. We will see that while the Holy Spirit does not give new doctrine or add to the Scriptures, he *does* guide us personally in our lives. Just as he led Philip, so the Holy Spirit leads us to carry the flame of God's love to the people around us—men and women who are often wide open to the gospel and just waiting for us to come along and speak it into their lives.

Connect | 15 MINUTES

Get the session started by choosing one of the following questions to discuss as a group:

- What is something that spoke to your heart in last week's personal study that you would like to share with the group?

— *or* —

- When has the Holy Spirit prompted you to say or do something?

Watch | 20 MINUTES

Now watch the video for this session. Below is an outline of the key points covered during the teaching. Record any key concepts that stand out to you.

Outline

I. Persecution in the early church led to the flame being carried to Judea and Samaria.
  A. The persecution broke out after the martyrdom of Stephen (see Acts 8:1–3).
  B. The believers didn't preach sermons but just told others what Jesus had done in their lives.
  C. In the early church, it was sheep multiplying sheep.

II. Philip was a deacon and one of the people who had fled from Jerusalem.
  A. Philip ended up in Samaria and began to share the gospel (see Acts 8:4–8).
  B. The Holy Spirit did amazing miracles through Philip (see Acts 8:9–25).
  C. In the midst of this revival, an angel told Philip to go to a desert road (see Acts 8:26).

III. As Philip stood on the desert road, God arranged a meeting for him with a eunuch who worked for the queen of Ethiopia.
  A. The Holy Spirit told Philip to go up to the chariot and stay near it (see Acts 8:27–29).
  B. When Philip obeyed, the Lord opened a door for him to share the gospel with the eunuch.
  C. Philip's obedience led to the eunuch being saved and, according to tradition, taking the gospel to Africa (see Acts 8:30–40).

IV. How did the gospel go to Africa? The Holy Spirit spoke to Philip and led him to the eunuch.
  A. Do you believe that the Holy Spirit can still speak to people?
  B. The Holy Spirit doesn't speak new doctrine or anything that contradicts Scripture, but he does guide us personally.
  C. Don't we need the Holy Spirit to speak to us today and lead us as we serve him?

V. God has chosen to use ordinary people to carry the flame of the gospel to others.
  A. Let's take an honest look inside of ourselves and at the churches we attend.
  B. Is what's happening in our lives and churches the best that God has for us?
  C. Let's ask God for more of his Holy Spirit. He has promised to give him to us.

Notes

Discuss | 35 MINUTES

Take some time to discuss what you just watched by answering the following questions. The suggested questions below will help you begin your discussion, but feel free to pick any of the additional questions as well as time allows.

Suggested Questions

1. In every place the early believers were scattered, they carried the flame, telling people the good news about Jesus and what he had done. How does this compare to what you see in the church today? Do you think this kind of revival still takes place?

2. Philip ended up in Samaria. What did the Holy Spirit do through him as he shared the gospel with the people there—whom the Jews usually hated (see Acts 8:5–8)?

3. In the midst of a vibrant ministry in Samaria, God instructed Philip to leave his work there and go off to a desert road. When has God asked you to do something that didn't make sense to you at first? How did you respond to his leading?

4. Do you believe that the Holy Spirit still speaks to people? Explain your response. What stories in the New Testament can you think of (besides Philip's) that the ways in which the Holy Spirit speaks to people and guides their steps?

Additional Questions

5. The believers who carried the flame to Judea and Samaria didn't carry a diploma from a seminary or an ordination document with them. They didn't worry about their qualifications. They simply shared how Jesus had transformed their lives. What does this tell us about the power of the gospel and the types of people that God uses?

6. Philip likely didn't understand why the Holy Spirit was directing him to travel to a desert road in Gaza, but he obeyed and went any way. Because of his obedience, he got to take part in a God-ordained encounter with the Ethiopian eunuch. When was a time that God clearly arranged circumstances and led you, as he did Philip, to minister to someone else?

7. Consider this statement: "The Christian church can't be organized into victory. It has to be led and anointed by the Holy Spirit into a position of bearing much fruit for our Lord." What does it mean that the church can't be "organized" into victory when it comes to carrying the flame? Why is anointing of the Holy Spirit necessary?

8. Read Luke 11:12–13. All of us make excuses as to why we can't be used by God to share his love with others—we're too old, we're too young, we're not trained, we're not eloquent to lead someone to Christ. But what radical promise does Jesus make in this passage? What is required on our part for the Holy Spirit to give us the words to say?

Respond | 10 MINUTES

Take a few moments to reflect on the final message from this session that God is looking for people who, like Philip, are willing and ready to go whenever he calls them—to wherever he leads. Review the outline for the video teaching and any notes you took. Use the following questions to write down your most significant takeaways from this session.

What spoke most to your heart from the video teaching?

What do you sense God is stirring you to do as a result?

What are your next steps when it comes to following the Holy Spirit's leading?

Pray | 10 MINUTES

End your time by praying together. Ask the Lord to lead you into situations in the upcoming week where you, like Philip, can share the message of God's love to those who are in need. Ask if anyone has prayer requests to share, and then write those requests in the space below so that you and your members can continue to pray about them in the weeks ahead.

Name | Request

PERSONAL STUDY

Congratulations! You have reached the last personal study. As you heard in this week's teaching, all that is required for you to *carry the flame* of God's love is to be open and obedient to the Holy Spirit's leading. This week, you will have the chance to look at a few passages of Scripture that reveal how the Holy Spirit speaks to you and guides you in your service to him. As you complete these exercises, be sure to write down your responses in the space provided and share your insights with a fellow group member if you are doing this study with others.

DAY 1

TALKING ABOUT JESUS

Sometimes bad situations lead to good results. At least, that is what happened when the early church in Jerusalem suffered persecution at the hands of the Jewish religious leaders and were scattered throughout the regions of Judea and Samaria. Despite being forced to flee from their homes, these believers "preached the word wherever they went" (Acts 8:4). The gospel was finally being spread beyond Jerusalem—which had been Jesus' plan all along (see Acts 1:8).

The Greek word for *preached* doesn't always mean speaking formally from a pulpit, like a pastor does. It simply means "to bring good news."[18] The early believers were not preaching sermons . . . remember, they didn't even have the New Testament yet! They were just telling people the basics of the gospel and what Jesus had done to change their lives.

We don't need to know every verse in the Bible or have a seminary degree to share the love of Jesus. We just need to know a few things: (1) Jesus died to pay the price for our sin, (2) he defeated death when he rose from the grave, and (3) if we turn to him and repent of our sins, he will forgive us and give us eternal life. When we tell people this good news and add our own stories of how Jesus saved us from darkness and brought us into the light, the Holy Spirit can use our simple testimonies to touch people's hearts.

The early Christians talked about Jesus everywhere they went. Do we do the same? More often than not, we talk about things like a great movie we saw or an exciting football game we attended or a new car we bought. These are all good things, but if these topics dominate our conversations, our focus might be off center.

When we are filled with the Holy Spirit and walking closely with the Lord, we will want to talk about Jesus. This doesn't mean that we should knock people over with the gospel or push them into spiritual discussions. It just means that if Jesus is on our minds and hearts, we will constantly be listening for his Holy Spirit's leading as we look for opportunities to share Christ with others.

Read | Acts 8:1–4, Philippians 1:12–14, and Romans 10:14–15

Reflect

1. The book of Acts records that after the martyrdom of Stephen, who was accused of blasphemy by the Jewish religious leaders and put to death (see Acts 7:54–58), a great persecution broke out in Jerusalem that caused the rank-and-file believers to flee the city. While this could have made these early believers afraid to share the message of the gospel, it actually fueled the flame for them (see Acts 8:4). How does Philippians 1:12–14 shed more light on this?

2. Jesus had told his followers that when the Holy Spirit came on them, they would be his witness "in Jerusalem, and in all Judea and Samaria, and to the ends of the earth" (Acts 1:8). Why do you think it took persecution to finally move them to take the gospel to other parts of the world? How ready are you to take the gospel to people outside your comfort zone?

3. Paul's words in Romans 10:14–15 are often applied to missionaries or pastors, but they can also apply to any believer who is sent by Jesus to take the gospel to others. How does this passage reveal the Lord's heart toward those who take the good news of Christ those who had not heard it?

4. If you brought the good news of the gospel to someone, what would you tell him or her? In other words, how has Jesus changed your life?

Pray | End your time in prayer. Thank the Lord for his gift of salvation and ask him to help you talk about him wherever you go.

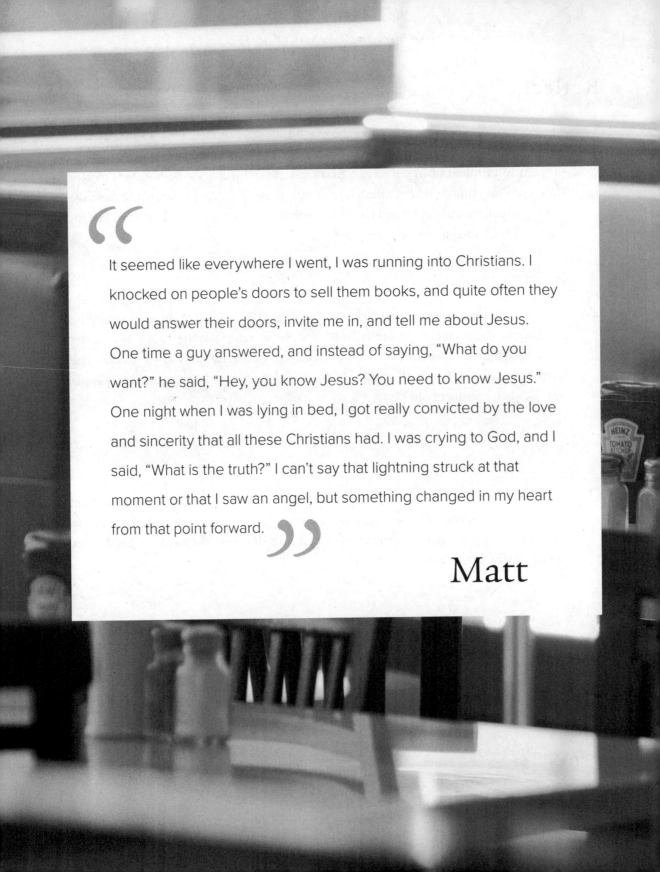

"It seemed like everywhere I went, I was running into Christians. I knocked on people's doors to sell them books, and quite often they would answer their doors, invite me in, and tell me about Jesus. One time a guy answered, and instead of saying, "What do you want?" he said, "Hey, you know Jesus? You need to know Jesus." One night when I was lying in bed, I got really convicted by the love and sincerity that all these Christians had. I was crying to God, and I said, "What is the truth?" I can't say that lightning struck at that moment or that I saw an angel, but something changed in my heart from that point forward."

Matt

DAY 2
AN OBEDIENT HEART

Jesus is not just our Savior but he is also our Lord. If we want to serve him effectively, we have to be ready to obey him. As we have seen this week, Philip, one of the believers who was scattered from Jerusalem by persecution, is a great example of someone who was ready to do whatever the Lord asked.

For starters, Philip went to a city in Samaria . . . to a group of people that most Jews avoided. The Samaritans were a blend of Jew and Gentile and had a mixed version of worship toward God that had come down to them from idolatrous forefathers. Most Jews, even ones who were believers in Jesus, didn't feel much love for the Samaritans (see Luke 9:51–55). But Philip, like Jesus, went to people outside his circle in order to take them the gospel.

When Philip proclaimed the gospel in Samaria, the people "paid close attention to what he said" (Acts 8:6). Remember that Philip was not a pastor or a preacher; his job in the Jerusalem church had been handing out food to the widows in the congregation. But God now did amazing miracles through him—casting demons out of people, healing the sick, and bringing men and women to salvation.

In the midst of all this excitement, an angel of the Lord told Philip, "Go south to the road—the desert road—that goes down from Jerusalem to Gaza" (verse 26). There was no further explanation or guidance provided . . . just an instruction to "go to the desert road."

Leave a thriving revival and go to Nowheresville? And do what there? You and I would probably have wanted a few more details.

But Philip wasn't concerned with particulars. He just wanted to put himself at God's disposal. He understood what F.B. Meyer wrote centuries later: "Christ must be Master. His will must rule, though it seems to contradict the dearest traditions of the soul."[19]

Oh, that God would give us all hearts like that! When we are wide open to the Holy Spirit's leading, God will position us to be used by him more powerfully than we could ever orchestrate or imagine.

Read | Acts 8:4–8, 12–26; John 14:23; Luke 6:46–49

Reflect

1. Because of Philip's obedience to be the Lord's witness in Samaria, a place the Jewish people normally avoided, what were at least three results that occurred in people's lives (see Acts 8:7–8)?

2. A man named Simon, who practiced sorcery in Samaria, was so impressed by the power of the Holy Spirit that flowed through ordinary believers that he tried to buy the gift with money. How did Peter respond to his request? What did Peter say was actually needed in order to receive this power from God (see Acts 8:18–23)?

3. Sometimes God will ask us to do things that make no sense to us in the moment—such as leave what we perceive to be a powerful work of God to go to someplace that has no possibilities. How might the Lord's guidance like this be a test of our faith? According to John 14:23, how will God reward our faithful obedience to him?

4. Jesus states in Luke 6:46 that it is possible for us to call him "Lord" yet not actually obey him. What does Jesus go on to say will happen to the person who truly obeys the Lord with his or her whole heart? How does this passage both challenge and encourage you in your journey with Christ?

Pray | End your time in prayer. Thank the Lord that he wants to use you, and ask him to help you put yourself fully at his disposal for anything he might ask of you.

DAY 3
DIVINE APPOINTMENTS

God has plans for us beyond anything that we could ever imagine. When an angel of the Lord told Philip to go to a desert road in the region of Gaza, Philip had no idea what God had in mind. But as he obediently walked along that wilderness track, he saw an Ethiopian eunuch in a chariot. That's when the Holy Spirit gave Philip the next step: "Go to that chariot and stay near it" (Acts 8:29). Philip ran up to the chariot and heard the eunuch reading from the Old Testament.

The life of a eunuch—a slave who could never have a family of his own—would have been lonely. Interestingly, the eunuch was reading a passage from Isaiah 53, which speaks of the Messiah being deprived of his life and leaving behind no descendants. Perhaps the grief and injustice the Ethiopian eunuch saw in this prophecy from the Old Testament resonated with his own heart.

Philip approached the man and asked if he understood what he was reading. The eunuch replied, "How can I, unless someone explains it to me?" (Acts 8:31). Talk about an open door! The eunuch invited Philip to come up into his chariot and then said, "Tell me please, who is the prophet talking about, himself or someone else?" (verse 35). Beginning there, Philip told this man about Jesus.

Next, "as they traveled along the road, they came to some water" (verse 36). The eunuch asked to be baptized, and when the two men came up out of the water, the eunuch went on his way rejoicing (see verses 37–39). Whatever had been on his heart before this moment, he was now filled with joy. As discussed in this week's group time, tradition tells us that he then took the gospel back to Ethiopia, where it spread among the nation.

We don't know what others need, but Jesus does. As Andrew Murray wrote, "The Lord Jesus Christ is the author and leader of missions. Whoever stands right with Him and abides in Him will be ready to know and do His will."[20] As you walk closely with Jesus, he will lead you in paths you didn't even know were there and will use you powerfully for his glory.

Read | Acts 8:26–39, Proverbs 16:9, and John 15:12–15

Reflect

1. After Philip followed the prompting of the Holy Spirit, "he met an Ethiopian eunuch, an important official in charge of all the treasury of the Kandake (which means 'queen of the Ethiopians')" (Acts 8:27). Clearly, this man was an influential official in his country, and there is no way that Philip would have otherwise encountered him. When has God likewise arranged a divine appointment for you or someone you know to share his love with someone else? What happened as a result?

2. According to Proverbs 16:9, we can make plans for ourselves, but it is the Lord who directs our steps. How is the Lord directing your steps today? What step of obedience do you need to take that can position you to hear the Lord's next instruction?

3. Andrew Murray wrote that "whoever stands right with Him and abides in Him will be ready to know and do His will." How does this describe your walk with Jesus?

4. In John 15:15, Christ told his followers that he no longer considered them to be servants but friends. If you are a friend of Jesus, he will speak to you by his Holy Spirit and show you his will. How does this encourage you as you seek to serve the Lord?

Pray | End your time in prayer. Thank the Lord for guiding you and ask him to make you sensitive and obedient to his voice as he leads you to divine appointments.

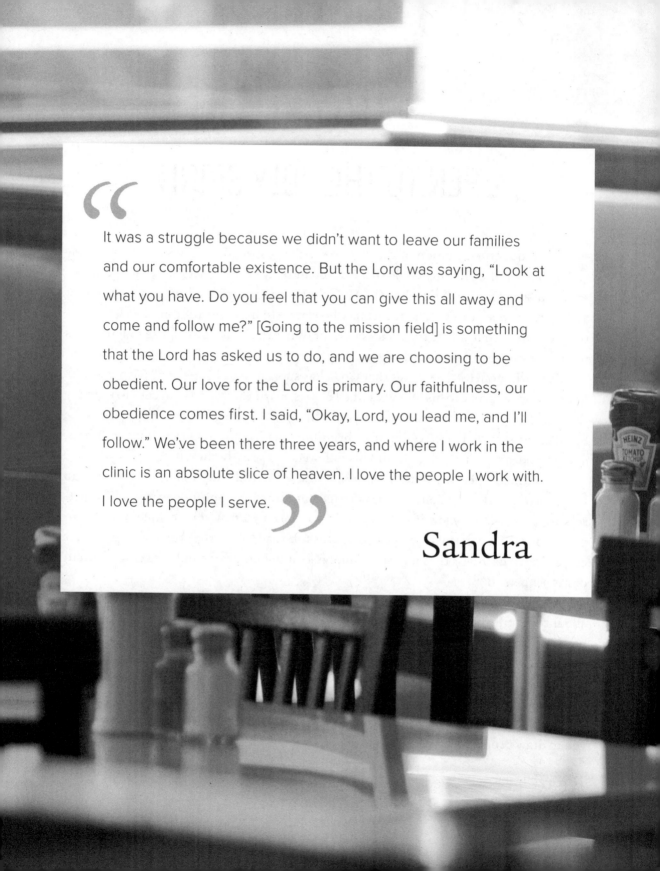

"It was a struggle because we didn't want to leave our families and our comfortable existence. But the Lord was saying, "Look at what you have. Do you feel that you can give this all away and come and follow me?" [Going to the mission field] is something that the Lord has asked us to do, and we are choosing to be obedient. Our love for the Lord is primary. Our faithfulness, our obedience comes first. I said, "Okay, Lord, you lead me, and I'll follow." We've been there three years, and where I work in the clinic is an absolute slice of heaven. I love the people I work with. I love the people I serve."

Sandra

DAY 4

OPEN TO THE HOLY SPIRIT

How does the tradition of the church say the gospel got to Ethiopia? By the Holy Spirit telling Philip, "Go to that chariot and stay near it" (Acts 8:29). Notice in this simple instruction to Philip that the Holy Spirit was not giving him new doctrine or adding to the Scriptures. In fact, anyone who claims to have a word from the Holy Spirit that adds to or contradicts the Bible is in error. What the Holy Spirit spoke to Philip was not new doctrine. It was a word of *guidance*.

The author of Hebrews states that God "has spoken to us by his Son" (Hebrews 1:2). Jesus, of course, spoke to his followers when he was on the earth, and he speaks to us today through the Bible. But he also speaks to us by his Spirit! Remember, the Holy Spirit is the Spirit of Jesus (see Acts 16:7; Galatians 4:6; Philippians 1:19). The Spirit is Jesus within us, and he guides us today just as he did his followers in the early church.

Some Christians believe that because we have the full canon of Scripture, it is no longer necessary for the Spirit to speak to us. But if the Holy Spirit doesn't guide us personally, how will we know if God wants us to move to a new state or marry a certain person or take a particular job—or go to a desert road? Even the Word of God cannot come alive to us unless the Holy Spirit impresses it on our hearts and speaks its truth to our inner person.

Yes, the Holy Spirit speaks to us today. However, as we discussed when we talked about being filled with the Spirit, we need *balance*. We should not be led by our own impressions or emotions into unbiblical persuasions, but neither should we be so afraid of error that we miss the Spirit's genuine leading—to reach out to someone, write a letter, ask forgiveness, help a stranger.

Do you believe in the Holy Spirit, not just doctrinally, but also in your heart? Are you completely yielded to his leading in your life? Open your heart to him—and he will use you to draw people to Jesus.

Read | 2 Timothy 3:16–17, Hebrews 1:1–2, and John 10:3–5

Reflect

1. The apostle Paul states that Scripture is "God-breathed and is useful for teaching, rebuking, correcting and training in righteousness" (1 Timothy 3:16). God doesn't give us new doctrine, because Scripture is complete. However, he does give us personal guidance through his Word and by his Spirit. What is the difference between new revelation and personal guidance?

2. According to Hebrews 1:2, in these last days God has spoken to us by his Son, Jesus. What are some ways that Jesus speaks to us? What are some of the ways that you have experienced Jesus speaking to you?

3. Jesus said that his sheep know his voice and will not follow the voice of a stranger (see John 10:3–5). When we think God is leading us to do something, how can we be sure that the leading is from him and not our own feelings or someone else's influence?

4. Don't we need to follow the personal leading of the Holy Spirit today as much as the first believers in Jesus did? If every believer today was open to the Spirit's guidance, what difference do you think it would make in the impact we have on this world?

Pray | End your time in prayer. Thank God that he speaks to each of us today through his Holy Spirit, and ask him to make you more sensitive to his voice.

DAY 5
COME, HOLY SPIRIT

Picture the Holy Spirit being poured out on the 120 believers gathered together in a prayer meeting in Jerusalem. Picture the Holy Spirit empowering Barnabas with the gift of encouragement so that he could sacrificially help other believers in need. Picture the Holy Spirit telling Philip to stay near the chariot of a lonely man who needed Jesus. Now picture your life and your church today. What would it be like if the Holy Spirit had his way among his people?

As we have noted, Jesus didn't suffer and die on the cross and rise again on the third day just so we could go to church on Sundays and receive instruction. No, God wants to fill us and empower us every day so that he can use us to draw unsaved people to Jesus and grow believers to maturity in Christ. After all, as Peter said in his sermon on the Day of Pentecost, "In the last days, God says, I will pour out my Spirit on all people" (Acts 2:17).

Some believers today are walking in the power of the Spirit and ministering to others in his power. But sadly, many are not. So, as you come to the close of this study, ask yourself what Jesus is calling you to do. Are you fulfilling that call in the power and authority of his Holy Spirit, or are you holding back? What would happen if we all began to pray the words of this old song?

> Come, Holy Spirit, we need you;
> Come, sweet Spirit, I pray.
> Come in your strength and your power.
> Come in your own gentle way.[21]

Jesus said that if we ask the Father for the Holy Spirit, he will give him to us (see Luke 11:13). But are we asking? We don't want to fall into fanaticism, but neither do we want a dead life that does nothing to change hearts or build God's kingdom. So let's put away our excuses. Let's ask God to send his Holy Spirit and fill us again today. As we do, God will revive us, and he will use us to carry the flame of his love and light to a world in desperate need.

Read | Matthew 28:16–20, Acts 2:17–18, and Luke 11:9–13

Reflect

1. When Jesus was preparing to leave this world and ascend into heaven, he gave these instructions to his followers: "Go and make disciples of all nations, baptizing them in the name of the Father and of the Son and of the Holy Spirit" (Matthew 28:19). What does this reveal about Jesus' purposes for dying on the cross and rising from the dead? In other words, what is his purpose for his church (see also Acts 1:8)?

2. How does the promise of Acts 2:17–18 challenge you? How does it encourage you?

3. Are you living out the best God has for you? What excuses or fears do you need to lay aside in order to better follow the leading of the Holy Spirit?

4. When was the last time that you asked Jesus to fill you with his Spirit? How do the promises of Luke 11:9–13 encourage you to persistently and expectantly ask the Lord for his Holy Spirit?

Pray | End your time in prayer. Thank the Lord for the promise of his Holy Spirit, and ask him to fill you again that you might carry his light and love to the world around you.

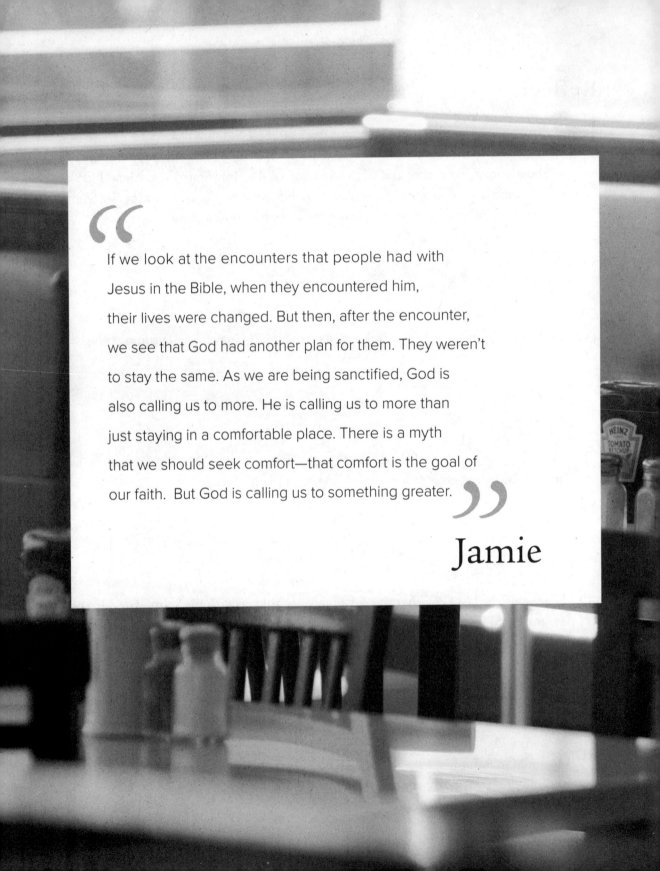

"

If we look at the encounters that people had with
Jesus in the Bible, when they encountered him,
their lives were changed. But then, after the encounter,
we see that God had another plan for them. They weren't
to stay the same. As we are being sanctified, God is
also calling us to more. He is calling us to more than
just staying in a comfortable place. There is a myth
that we should seek comfort—that comfort is the goal of
our faith. But God is calling us to something greater.

"

Jamie

LEADER'S GUIDE

Thank you for your willingness to lead your group through this study! What you have chosen to do is valuable and will make a great difference in the lives of others. *Carry the Flame* is a five-session Bible study built around video content and small-group interaction. As the group leader, imagine yourself as the host of a party. Your job is to take care of your guests by managing the details so that when your guests arrive, they can focus on one another and on the interaction around the topic for that session.

Your role as the group leader is not to answer all the questions or reteach the content—the video and study guide will do most of that work. Your job is to guide the experience and cultivate your small group into a connected and engaged community. This will make it a place for members to process, question, and reflect—not necessarily receive more instruction. There are several elements in this leader's guide that will help you as you structure your study and reflection time, so be sure to follow along and take advantage of each one.

Before You Begin

Before your first meeting, make sure the group members have a copy of this study guide. Alternately, you can hand out the study guides at your first meeting and give the members some time to look over the material and ask any preliminary questions. Also make sure they are aware that they have access to the streaming videos at any time by following the instructions printed on the inside front cover. During your first meeting, ask the members to provide their name, phone number, and e-mail address so you can keep in touch with them.

Generally, the ideal size for a group is eight to ten people, which will ensure that everyone has enough time to participate in discussions. If you have more people, you might want to break up the main group into smaller subgroups. Encourage those who show up at the first meeting to commit to attending the duration of the study, as this will help the group members get to know one another, create stability for the group, and help you know how best to prepare to lead the participants through the material.

Each session begins with an opening reflection in the Welcome section. The questions that follow in the Connect section serve as an icebreaker to get the group members thinking about the topic. Some people may want to tell a long story in response to one of these questions, but the goal is to keep the answers brief. Ideally, you want everyone in the group to get a chance to answer, so try to keep the responses to a minute or less. If you have talkative group members, say up front that everyone needs to limit their answer to one minute.

Give the group members a chance to answer, but also tell them to feel free to pass if they wish. With the rest of the study, it's generally not a good idea to have everyone answer every question—a free-flowing discussion is more desirable. But with the opening icebreaker questions, you can go around the circle. Encourage shy people to share, but don't force them.

At your first meeting, let the group members know each session contains a personal study section they can use to continue to engage with the content until the next meeting. While this is optional, it will help them cement the concepts presented during the group study time. Let them know that if they choose to do so, they can watch the video for the next session by accessing the streaming code found on the inside front cover of their studies. Invite them to bring any questions and insights to your next meeting, especially if they had a breakthrough moment or didn't understand something.

Preparation for Each Session

As the leader, there are a few things you should do to best prepare for each meeting:

- **Read through the session.** This will help you become more familiar with the content and know how to structure the discussion times.

- **Decide how the videos will be used.** Determine whether you want the members to watch the videos ahead of time (again, via the streaming access code found on the study's inside front cover) or together as a group.

- **Decide which questions you want to discuss.** Based on the length of your group discussions, you may not be able to get through all the questions. So look over the recommendations for the suggested and additional questions in each session, and mark which ones you definitely want to cover.

- **Be familiar with the questions you want to discuss.** When the group meets, you'll be watching the clock, so make sure you are familiar with the questions you have selected. In this way, you will ensure that you have the material more deeply in your mind than your group members.

- **Pray for your group.** Pray for your group members and ask God to lead them as they study his Word and listen to his Spirit.

In many cases there will be no one "right" answer to the question. Answers will vary, especially when group members are being asked to share their personal experiences.

Structuring the Discussion Time

You will need to determine with your group how long you want to meet so you can plan your time accordingly. Suggested times for each section have been provided in this study guide, and if you adhere to these times, your group will meet for ninety minutes. If you want to meet for two hours, follow the times given in the right-hand column:

Section	90 Minutes	120 Minutes
CONNECT (discuss one or more of the opening questions for the session)	15 minutes	20 minutes
WATCH (watch the teaching material together and take notes)	20 minutes	20 minutes
DISCUSS (discuss the study questions you selected ahead of time)	35 minutes	50 minutes
RESPOND (write down key takeaways)	10 minutes	15 minutes
PRAY (pray together and dismiss)	10 minutes	15 minutes

As the group leader, it is up to you to keep track of the time and to keep things on schedule. You might want to set a timer for each segment so that both you and the group members know when the time is up. Don't be concerned if group members are quiet or slow to share. People are often quiet when they are pulling together their ideas, and this might be a new experience for some of them. Just ask a question and let it hang in the air until someone shares. You can then say, "Thank you. What about others? What came to you when you watched that portion of the teaching?"

Group Dynamics

Leading a group through *Carry the Flame* will prove to be highly rewarding both to you and your group members. But you still may encounter challenges along the way! Discussions can get off track. Group members may not be sensitive to the needs and ideas of others. Some might worry that they will be expected to talk about matters that make them feel awkward. Others may express comments that result in disagreements. To help ease this strain on you and the group, consider the following ground rules:

- When someone raises a question or comment that is off the main topic, suggest that you deal with it another time, or, if you feel led to go in that direction, let the group know that you will be spending some time discussing it.

- If someone asks a question that you don't know how to answer, admit it, and move on. At your discretion, feel free to invite group members to comment on questions that call for personal experience.

- If you find that one or two people are dominating the discussion time, direct a few questions to others in the group. Outside the main group time, ask the more dominating members to help you draw out the quieter ones. Work to make them part of the solution instead of considering them part of the problem.

- When a disagreement occurs, encourage the group members to process the matter in love. Encourage those on opposite sides to restate what they heard the other side say about the matter, and then invite each side to evaluate if that perception is accurate. Lead the group in examining other scriptures related to the topic, and look for common ground.

When any of these issues arise, encourage your group members to follow these words from Scripture: "Love one another" (John 13:34); "If it is possible, as far as it depends on you, live at peace with everyone" (Romans 12:18); and, "Be quick to listen, slow to speak and slow to become angry" (James 1:19). This will make your group time more rewarding and beneficial for everyone who attends.

Thank you again for taking the time to lead your group. You are making a difference in your group members' lives and having an impact on their journey toward understanding what it means to to carry the flame of the gospel into a world that needs God's love.

ABOUT THE AUTHOR

J im Cymbala was born in Brooklyn, New York, where he enjoyed a successful career playing basketball in high school and then college. Upon graduation from the University of Rhode Island, he entered the business world and married his childhood sweetheart, Carol. Although unforeseen by them, it wasn't long before God called them into ministry.

Arriving at The Brooklyn Tabernacle, Pastor Cymbala and Carol found a congregation of less than twenty people meeting in a rundown building located in an impoverished part of downtown Brooklyn. Over the years, God has shown his faithfulness to them and their congregation in many miraculous ways. Their present campus includes a large, renovated theater in downtown Brooklyn, where thousands of people come each week to hear the good news of Jesus.

Pastor Cymbala is the author of several books, including the bestselling *Fresh Wind, Fresh Fire*, which was named Christian Book of the Year. He has also done a number of video series on prayer and other important topics for the Christian church, including *When God's Spirit Moves, Life-Changing Prayer,* and *Spiritual Warfare Is Real.* His wife, Carol, directs the six-time Grammy Award Winning Brooklyn Tabernacle Choir, whose music has blessed people around the world.

ENDNOTES

1. Some translations say that Jesus sent out *seventy-two* people: "After this the Lord appointed seventy-two others" (Luke 10:1 NIV). The discrepancy in the number (70 or 72) is due to the differences found in the ancient scrolls used for the translation, the texts of which are nearly evenly divided between the numbers.
2. Hudson Taylor (1832–1905), cited in J. C. Pollock, *Hudson Taylor and Maria: Pioneers in China* (Eastbourne, East Sussex, UK: Kingsway, 1983).
3. Jim Cymbala, *You Were Made for More* (Grand Rapids, MI: Zondervan, 2008), 24.
4. Lettie Cowman (1870–1960), *Streams in the Desert* (Los Angeles,CA: Oriental Missionary Society, 1925), July 30.
5. A.B. Simpson (1843–1919), *The Life of Prayer* and *The Power of Stillness* (Scotts Valley, CA: CreateSpace, 2010), 18.
6. Harold Vaughan, *Approaching God's Throne: Biblical Protocols for Prayer* (Vinton, VA: Christ Life Publications, 2019), ix.
7. In Acts 4:36, the Greek word used for "of encouragement" is *paraklēseōs*. In John 14:16, the Greek word used for the Holy Spirit (variously translated as advocate, helper, comforter, counselor) is *paraklēton*. The word comes from the root *pará*, "from close beside," and *kaléō*, "to make a call." In New Testament times, it generally referred to an attorney who gave evidence on behalf of a client that stood up in court.
8. Samuel Chadwick (1860–1932), *The Way to Pentecost* (Berne, IN: Light and Hope Publications, 1937).
9. Andrew Murray (1828–1917), *The Full Blessing of Pentecost* (Fort Washington, PA: CLC, 2005).
10. A.W. Tozer (1897–1963), *How to Be Filled with the Holy Spirit* (Camp Hill, PA: Christian Publications, 1991), 19.
11. Tozer, *How to Be Filled with the Holy Spirit*, 39–40.
12. The Greek word for "be filled" in Ephesians 5:18 is *plērousthe*. It is in the imperative mood, which means that Paul here is issuing a command. *Plērousthe* is also in the present tense (not the past tense), which indicates the filling of the Holy Spirit is an ongoing process. We are to be *continuously* filled with the Spirit. See Warren W. Wiersbe, *Be Rich, Ephesians* (Wheaton, IL: Victor Books, 1976), 136.
13. David Guzik, "Ephesians 5—Life in the Spirit," Enduring Word, accessed December 16, 2022, https://enduringword.com/bible-commentary/ephesians-5/.
14. D.L. Moody (1837–1899), *Secret Power* (New Kensington, PA: Whitaker, 1997), 107–108.
15. Leonardo Blair, "Most Adult US Christians Don't Believe Holy Spirit Is Real: Study," Christian Post, September 10, 2021, https://www.christianpost.com/news/most-us-christians-dont-believe-holy-spirit-is-real-study.html.
16. A.B. Simpson (1843–1919), *The Holy Spirit or Power from On High*, volume 2, chapter 15, Worthy Christian Books, accessed December 16, 2022, https://worthychristianbooks.com/ab-simpson/chapter-15-all-the-blessings-of-the-spirit-or-the-holy-ghost-in-ephesians/.
17. E.M. Bounds (1835–1913), *Power Through Prayer* (Chicago, IL: Moody Publishers, 2009).
18. The Greek word *euangelizō* is used in Scripture to describe the act of: (1) bringing good news or announcing glad tidings; (2) announcing especially the glad tidings of the coming kingdom of God and of the salvation to be obtained through Christ; and (3) instructing people of the things that pertain to salvation. See Blue Letter Bible, s.v. "Euangelizō," https://www.blueletterbible.org/lexicon/g2097/KJV/tr/0-1/.
19. F.B. Meyer (1847–1929), *Peter* (Fort Washington, PA: CLC, 2002).
20. Andrew Murray, *The Key to the Missionary Problem* (Fort Washington, PA: CLC, 2007).
21. Bill and Gloria Gaither, "Come Holy Spirit We Need You," 1964.

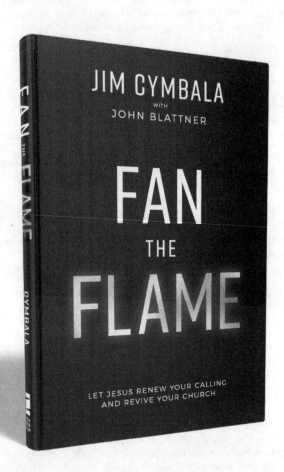